The Art And Science Of Herding Cats

THE ART AND SCIENCE OF HERDING CATS

INFLUENCE, IDENTITY, AND LEADERSHIP IN THE AGE OF AI

Deepa Kartha

Copyright © 2026 by Deepa Kartha

All rights reserved.

No part of this book may be reproduced, distributed, or transmitted in any form or by any means, including photocopying, recording, or other electronic or mechanical methods, without the prior written permission of the author, except in the case of brief quotations used in reviews or scholarly work.

Paperback ISBN: 979-8-9952849-1-8

eBook ISBN: 979-8-9952849-0-1

Published independently.

First Edition.

Typeset by YouTbooks

The views and opinions expressed in this book are those of the author and do not necessarily reflect those of any organizations referenced.

For more information, visit: **DeepaKartha.com**

Dedication

For those who have ever tried to herd cats and discovered something deeper about people along the way.

Contents

ACKNOWLEDGMENTS

Before the ideas in this book took shape, many people shaped how I learned to observe the world, ask questions, and pay closer attention to human behavior. I am deeply grateful to them.

Growing up with my nose deeply buried in books, I often heard my mother say something that stayed with me: "Deepa, you're floating through life. Pay attention."

At the time, I didn't fully understand what she meant. Like many people, I moved through life without noticing many of the patterns around me. Only later, especially after my children were born, did I begin to appreciate the depth of that simple advice: slow down, look more carefully, and notice what is happening beneath the surface.

To my father, who nurtured my curiosity about the world and encouraged a lifelong love of learning.

To my mother, whose reminder to pay attention continues to echo in ways I understand more deeply with time.

I am also deeply grateful to my teachers, Dr. Shivanand and Acharya Ishan Shivanananda. Through the practices of Shivyog, they introduced me to mindfulness, meditation, and inner observation. Those disciplines began the ongoing work of stepping outside my immediate reactions and learning to see situations with greater clarity and less judgment. That shift, still very much a work in progress, has shaped how I think about people, systems, and leadership.

To my husband, who has been my rock through my years in corporate America and through the journey of building something of my own, and through the many conversations and ideas that shaped this book. What shaped that perspective wasn't just working inside companies, but working across them as an entrepreneur. Engaging with customers across nonprofits, small businesses, and large organizations gave me a different lens. That experience taught me to see organizations not just as places where people work, but as living systems that shape behavior, choices, and influence every day.

To my children, each wonderfully unique in their own way. Watching the world through their curiosity has reminded me how many different ways there are to see, understand, and experience people and situations.

I am also grateful for the many conversations with my brother and with family members, friends, and colleagues whose perspectives deepened my fascination with human behavior. Even in moments when I was simply listening or observing quietly, I was often learning something about how people think, react, and influence one another.

Much of what appears in these pages grew out of those observations and conversations.

In the end, this book is simply an extension of that curiosity, an ongoing attempt, shaped by experience, to understand the systems, patterns, and human interactions unfolding around us every day.

Perhaps learning to lead, influence, and work with one another begins with something simpler than we often think.

It begins with paying attention.

I am grateful to everyone who has been part of that journey.

Preface

I've always been fascinated by history, and over time that became a habit of reading and following stories across time, not for the timelines or the famous leaders, but for the patterns hidden beneath them.

Not just what happened, but how leadership actually worked. How belief spread. How people moved together in certain directions while other ideas disappeared. How power shaped what felt normal, unquestionable, and inevitable.

And maybe most of all, why humanity seems determined to repeat the same mistakes with remarkable confidence.

Even when I started exploring leadership and corporate thinking, what struck me was how little of it was really 'corporate.' It almost always came back to human nature.

For a long time, that curiosity lived quietly in the background. I read. I noticed patterns. But like most people, I was busy juggling career, family, and the daily illusion that if we worked hard enough, we could control how things unfolded.

Things shifted when corporate leadership and motherhood showed up around the same time.

When you're responsible for other humans, at work or at home, theory becomes practical very quickly. You stop caring about what *should* work and start paying attention to what actually does. You notice how much your own behavior shapes the room around you. How small signals travel. How quickly things can shift from smooth coordination to complete confusion.

And how, despite our best intentions, control is far more limited than leadership myths would suggest.

At the time, I was deep in corporate life. Busy in the way that feels productive but leaves little room for reflection. I was leading teams, solving problems, moving quickly. But I wasn't connecting the dots.

That came later, when I started my own company.

Things slowed down just enough for patterns to surface. Meetings that went nowhere. Initiatives that quietly fizzled. People nodding along in the room and disengaging soon after. What I had seen for years suddenly began to align, not just with experience, but with history, psychology, and the behavior unfolding in real time around me.

Technology made those patterns impossible to ignore.

I've also long been interested in Big Tech, and as it began to take the world by storm, I found myself watching how quickly it became woven into everyday life. Social media, in particular, seemed to reshape how people interacted, what they paid attention to, and even how they felt about themselves. It was also making everything feel easier, more immediate, more comfortable, almost as if it was quietly pulling us into a different world altogether. You could see it in small but telling ways, packages showing up at our door with increasing frequency, interactions shifting onto screens, and attention being drawn more and more into these digital spaces. There was a kind of collective pull toward it that was hard to ignore. I watched this with a mix of curiosity and unease, including my own resistance to it. I found myself questioning why something as simple as a 'like' could carry so much emotional weight, why it could make someone feel validated, or not. It wasn't just about technology anymore. It was about how easily human behavior could be influenced, shaped, and amplified.

Around the same time, my inner work deepened.

My spiritual practice didn't give me answers so much as it trained my attention. It taught me to notice my reactions, my tendency to get swept up in momentum, and the stories shaping my choices. More than anything, it helped me see how easily I could be shaped by forces I barely noticed.

Once you learn to manage your own mind, something uncomfortable becomes obvious. Very few systems are designed to support clarity or long-term intention. Environments do most of the work. Incentives overpower willpower. People aren't failing. They're responding exactly the way the system trained them to.

That's when everything clicked.

History. Leadership. Technology. Teams. Culture. Algorithms.

Different contexts. Same dynamic.

Humans move through systems that shape behavior long before anyone thinks they're making a choice.

At first glance, a book about artificial intelligence might seem like an odd place to spend time talking about ancient history. But the deeper I looked, the more obvious something became.

The technology may be new. The mechanics are not.

Humans have always been influenced by systems that guide behavior. Pharaohs carved messages into temple walls. Roman leaders shaped public belief through spectacle and ritual. Newspapers, radio, and television each became the dominant influence engines of their time.

Today those forces live inside algorithms.

What once spread through temples, pamphlets, and stadiums now moves through personalized feeds, recommendation systems, and AI-driven platforms. The tools have changed. The speed has accelerated. But the underlying dynamics of influence remain remarkably familiar.

What *is* different today is the scale and velocity.

Artificial intelligence is rapidly reshaping how information spreads, how decisions are made, and how work gets done. Tasks that once required entire teams can now be completed by a single person working alongside intelligent tools. Ideas travel faster. Reactions spread faster. Influence operates at a speed we have never experienced before.

In an environment like this, something important becomes clear.

The more powerful our tools become, the more important human judgment becomes.

AI can amplify great thinking. It can also amplify confusion just as quickly.

Managing yourself becomes more important. Teams become more important. And perhaps most importantly, mindset becomes the real differentiator.

The question is no longer simply what tools we use.

It is how we think while using them.

AI will change many things about how work happens. But it does not change the fundamental nature of humans working together. Independent minds will still collide. Groups will still influence individual behavior. Systems will still shape decisions long before anyone consciously makes them.

In many ways, the age of AI simply makes these dynamics easier to see.

This book explores those dynamics.

It isn't a leadership manual. It isn't a critique of technology. And despite the title, it's not really about cats.

Cats are simply a useful metaphor.

Independent. Opinionated. Not particularly interested in being managed. Strangely predictable once you stop trying to control them directly.

Humans aren't all that different.

When independent minds gather in teams, organizations, communities, or digital spaces, behavior stops being linear. Influence becomes subtle.

Momentum forms and dissolves. A single signal can shift the direction of an entire room.

Plans still matter. Intentions still matter.

But systems often matter more.

This book doesn't try to fix that.

It simply makes the patterns visible.

Because once you start seeing how influence actually works in organizations, in technology, and in your own thinking, it becomes very hard to unsee.

And once you see those patterns, it becomes difficult to look at leadership, technology, and organizations the same way again.

That's where this conversation begins.

SECTION 1
IT'S THE STUPID ALGORITHMS

What shapes your thinking long before you notice.

You like to believe your thoughts are your own - original, deliberate, carefully formulated. But in reality most of what you think didn't start with you at all.

Since before first hieroglyph was carved, humans have been nudged, conditioned, persuaded, and guided by the same primitive mechanics: repetition, emotion, and selective messaging. And today, instead of stone walls and shouting crowds, those mechanics sit inside invisible algorithms that know what you'll click before you do.

This section is about the illusion of independent thought — how ideas are planted, repeated, reinforced, and finally absorbed without your permission. Ancient propaganda, Roman crowd manipulation, yellow journalism, social media feeds… it's all the same pattern microwaved and re-plated. Because once you understand how easily influence slips in, you'll see why it's so hard to escape — and why you often "think" things you never consciously chose.

Chapter 1

YOU THOUGHT YOU THOUGHT OF IT

"Nothing is more responsible for the good old days than a bad memory."
— Franklin Pierce Adams

There are two types of people in this world: the ones who swallow whatever information is handed to them like baby birds, and the ones who believe nothing enters their brain without a full forensic analysis.

Cute theory.

Not real.

Believing you're immune to influence is usually the first sign that you aren't.

Think about how many things you "knew" were true long before you could explain why. You have strong feelings about a brand you've never personally had a bad experience with. You "just know" it's terrible. Or overrated. Or elite.

How did you know?

All it takes for someone to believe almost anything is a simple formula, repeated often enough:

Repetition

The more often something is seen or heard, the more "true" it feels.

Emotion

Fear, anger, and hope are the fastest shortcuts into memory.

Selective messaging

Show the parts that fit the story and ignore the parts that don't.

This is a pattern humans have been falling for long before we had screens to blame. From billboards to pamphlets, telegrams to tweets, the mechanics haven't really changed since the time of the Pharaohs.

Repetition, emotion, selective messaging, the oldest technology we've got.

Pharaohs and the Influence Infrastructure

Long before hashtags, Egypt's Pharaohs ran one of history's most effective influence campaigns.

If you were an Egyptian citizen during the time of Ramesses II, disbelief would have been difficult.

Ramesses II built belief directly into the environment.

Temples and statues lined trade routes like sponsored posts, every carving showing him larger-than-life and eternally victorious. Priests reinforced the narrative through ritual and story, repeating it until doubt felt unnatural.

It was persuasion through infrastructure. You didn't just hear about the

Pharaoh's greatness. You lived inside it.

And if you saw all of this, you would likely believe Ramesses had decisively defeated the Hittites at Kadesh, even though the battle was far closer to a stalemate, because the story carved into stone outlasted the reality of the battle itself.

From Stone Walls to Social Walls

Fast-forward a few thousand years.

Where the Pharaoh carved belief into limestone, we carve it into pixels.

Today's temples of attention operate on the same ancient law: familiarity breeds belief.

Imagine you like grapes and walk into a grocery store looking for grapes. Now imagine the store stocks only grapes. After a while, you'd walk out convinced grapes are objectively superior fruit, not because you evaluated the full menu, but because the menu consisted only of grape varieties.

That's what algorithmic curation does. It narrows your reality to what you once liked or what the system believes people like you prefer.

The Modern Pharaoh Lives in Your Feed

Today's Pharaoh doesn't wear a crown. He lives in your feed.

His sculptors are coders. His priests are influencers. His temples are the glowing icons in our hands.

AI doesn't invent your beliefs, it personalizes them. It learns your fears, your cravings, your patterns, and feeds them back to you until the echo starts sounding like thought.

Certainty can arrive quickly when familiarity is constant.

When an Idea Feels Like Yours

I remember a school hack, adding "fying" to Indian words to make the nuns think we were speaking English. I could've sworn we invented it, until I realized everyone was doing it.

Did I think of it first, or did the idea spread so quietly that it simply felt like my own?

Influence doesn't knock first. It slips in through familiarity, repetition, and emotional resonance, until one day you find yourself defending a belief you never consciously chose.

Before You Turn the Page

Pattern

Ideas rarely arrive in isolation. What feels like independent thinking is often the result of repeated exposure, subtle influence, and familiar narratives shaping our perception.

Reflect on This

Which opinions do you feel most certain about?

Where did those ideas first come from?

Who reinforced them over time?

Pattern Interrupt

Choose one belief you hold strongly about work, leadership, or society. Ask two other people where they first encountered the same idea.

Notice whether the belief traces back to similar sources. Many of our "independent" thoughts travel along surprisingly similar paths.

Chapter 2

THE ALGORITHM OF YOUR REALITY

"Whenever you find yourself on the side of the majority,

it is time to pause and reflect."

— Mark Twain

Familiarity feels safe.

Repetition feels true.

Long before psychologists named the illusory truth effect, humans were already living inside echo chambers. Crowds, rituals, chants, symbols. Places where hearing the same thing repeatedly didn't just reinforce belief; it created it.

Echo chambers didn't begin with algorithms. They began with people.

With the comfort of hearing your own beliefs reflected back at you. With the emotional relief of knowing others saw the world the same way you did.

Over time, the architecture changed, from stadiums to newspapers, from television to personalized feeds, but the mechanism stayed the same.

We believe what we hear often enough, loudly enough, and from people who sound like us.

Rome: The Stadium-Sized Echo Chamber

Picture yourself in the Roman Colosseum, shoulder to shoulder with fifty thousand people. The roar. The chants. The banners. Repetition wasn't just something you heard, it was something you felt.

Romans believed the games reflected Roman virtue, discipline, dominance, sacrifice for the state. The message was staged, repeatedly, at scale.

Emperors sponsored the games.

Victories were announced, framed, and celebrated publicly.

The crowd learned when to cheer, when to jeer, when mercy was acceptable and when death was deserved.

Inside the Colosseum, belief wasn't explained. It was rehearsed.

Why Echo Chambers Feel So Good

Echo chambers aren't inherently malicious. They're psychological shortcuts. They give us identity, belonging, and certainty in a chaotic world.

And certainty is comforting.

Think about teams that pride themselves on being "driven" or "high-performing." The story becomes: we push hard because we care. Long hours and burnout are reframed as proof of commitment.

Echo chambers define what feels normal, what feels true, what feels widely accepted.

Certainty is addictive.

That's why teams cling to "how we do things here" long after it stops working.

Once something feels universally agreed upon inside your chamber, questioning it starts to feel like betrayal, not of an idea, but of your group.

Curiosity shrinks. Confidence hardens.

For a long time, this is how echo chambers worked, collectively. Shared spaces. Shared stories. Shared reinforcement.

When Echo Chambers Shrink

As media evolved, echo chambers didn't disappear. They got smaller. Sharper. More tailored. What once required a stadium now fits in your pocket.

Instead of crowds reinforcing a single narrative, algorithms reinforce your narrative, whatever keeps you engaged. Your digital world whispers the same ideas back to you until they stop sounding like opinions and start sounding like reality.

The modern echo chamber isn't loud.

It curates.

Every click becomes feedback. Every scroll trains the system to show you more of what already feels familiar.

Soon, your world starts to feel self-confirming, optimized by you, for you.

We don't just live in echo chambers anymore.

We carry them.

When certainty meets personalization, we stop noticing how much of our worldview was pre-selected. What feels like independent thinking is often reinforced familiarity.

The Selective Personalized Reality Problem

The most dangerous thing about modern echo chambers isn't misinformation. It's selective reality.

Two people can live in the same city, scroll the same platforms, and inhabit entirely different worlds, each convinced theirs is obvious and self-evident. Not because either is seeing more reality, but because each is seeing a different slice, served repeatedly until it feels complete.

The algorithm doesn't ask, Is this true?

It asks, Will this keep them here?

The longer you stay, the more your version of reality tightens.

Humans never stopped living in echo chambers.

We just upgraded them.

What was once the roar of thousands is now a whisper designed just for you — familiar, affirming, convincing.

And that's how something starts to feel like truth long before we question it.

PAUSE FOR A MOMENT

Pattern

What we believe is rarely formed in a vacuum. Invisible systems, social signals, and digital algorithms quietly shape what we see, think, and accept as reality.

Reflect on This

What sources shape your daily understanding of the world?

What perspectives rarely appear in your information stream?

Pattern Interrupt: Change the Feed

For the next three days, intentionally read or watch content from a credible voice outside your usual perspective.

Instead of debating it, simply observe what feels unfamiliar or uncomfortable.

Notice whether the discomfort comes from the argument itself or from hearing something different than usual.

Chapter 3

THE DECISION YOU DIDN'T MAKE

"We first make our habits, and then our habits make us."

—John Dryden

We aren't convinced by ideas.

We're convinced by ease.

Whatever requires the least effort gets repeated. Repetition becomes habit. Habit becomes outcome. And by the time we notice, the decision has already been made.

Convenience is the friendliest doorway into influence.

Humans choose the path of least resistance. If someone announced, "I'm about to influence your thinking," you'd brace yourself. But say, "I'll make this easier," and you lean back.

We don't resist convenience.

We move toward it.

Convenience shapes behavior more effectively than logic. The brain rewards shortcuts, builds habits around them, and defends those habits. Once an action becomes easy, the mind stops asking questions. Effort fades. Reflection disappears.

We're constantly making decisions, small ones, big ones, all the time. And every now and then, when one is made for us, it feels like a relief. I can't count the number of times I've thought: I wish someone would just decide this for me.

The Hidden Architecture of Ease

Years ago, Stanford researcher BJ Fogg mapped a simple behavior model: motivation, ability, and prompts. His insight was blunt, if you can't raise motivation, make the action easier. If ease isn't possible, lower the activation threshold.

That framework didn't stay in academia. It became the operating manual for product design.

Reduce friction.

Automate decisions.

Remove pauses.

Keep the user moving.

When friction disappears, reflection disappears with it.

As I was building my own platform, I saw these principles show up everywhere, reduce friction, automate decisions, remove pauses. But I found myself resisting parts of it. My goal wasn't to have people rely on the system. It was to help them focus on their work. And the more seamless the system became, the more that distinction started to blur.

One Click, Zero Thought

Amazon's one-click purchase removed a series of micro-decisions: Do I want this? Do I need it now? Should I wait? Each step once acted as a pause where doubt could surface.

The bumps disappeared. So did the pause.

Studies later confirmed the pattern: when effort drops, impulsive decisions rise. The design didn't just make shopping faster. It altered the rhythm of deciding. You didn't choose faster buying.

The system removed reconsideration.

Autoplay and the Vanishing Boundary

Netflix applied the same logic with autoplay. The missing pause between episodes erased the checkpoint where you decide whether to continue.

It feels harmless. But the absence of a boundary trains a habit. Researchers later linked binge cycles to disrupted sleep and increased anxiety.

We like to believe we chose three episodes.

Often, the design continued for us.

When Ease Becomes the Environment

Social platforms extend the pattern. Scrolling requires almost nothing. Reacting takes milliseconds. Content refreshes without end.

Ease becomes the hook.

The algorithm becomes the guide. Reinforcement becomes the habit.

Research on misinformation revealed something uncomfortable: false stories spread faster not because of intelligence gaps, but because they are easier, more emotional, more digestible, more shareable.

Convenience doesn't just tilt behavior.

It tilts truth.

The Mental Health Tax of Ease

The most subtle impact of convenience isn't on what we do, it's on how we think.

The brain evolved for effort followed by rest. Not constant stimulation. Not frictionless pathways. When everything becomes instant, certain capacities begin to erode:

our tolerance for slowness,

our ability to filter,

our capacity for boredom,

our comfort with uncertainty.

Convenience smooths the path for behavior, but it weakens psychological muscles, delaying gratification, choosing intentionally, sitting with discomfort.

These are foundations of emotional resilience.

Ease isn't harmful by default. But living entirely inside it reshapes us.

Designed to Herd

In the early 1900s, department stores installed escalators not just for comfort, but to guide movement. Shoppers carried along predefined paths browsed longer, and longer browsing correlated with increased purchasing.

Movement became guidance.

Ease became influence.

If an escalator could shape behavior a century ago, real-time systems fueled by behavioral data can do far more.

The Conveyor Belt of Modern Life

Convenience today isn't a staircase.

It's a conveyor belt.

Influence doesn't require pressure. It thrives in comfort. The softer the cushion, the subtler the guidance.

When technology anticipates your desires and removes the moments where you might second-guess yourself, the line between instinct and design blurs.

The more seamless the system, the more invisible the influence.

Convenience helps us.

It also invites us to hand over pieces of autonomy willingly.

And that's the part we don't notice.

A Small Check-In

The Pattern

Many decisions we believe we made consciously were actually shaped long before the moment of choice by context, expectations, and subtle nudges.

Reflect on This

Which parts of your day run on autopilot?

Where does convenience quietly replace intention?

Pattern Interrupt: Insert a Pause

Pick one habit you perform automatically. For the next week, pause for five seconds before doing it.

The pause is small but deliberate.

Notice how often awareness alone changes the behavior.

SECTION 2
WHEN THE ROOM FILLS WITH CATS

How Independent Thinkers Behave in Groups and How Chaos (or Genius) Emerges

There was a phrase that surfaced over the years, usually said with a half-smirk: "This feels like herding cats."

It appeared in moments when people were brought together by necessity rather than choice, cross-functional work, shared goals, time-bound efforts where alignment mattered but independence remained. Everyone involved was smart. Capable. Thoughtful. Yet once in the same room, outcomes became unpredictable.

What emerged wasn't resistance or lack of effort. It was interaction. Each person arrived with context, assumptions, priorities, and internal narratives. Individually, they made sense. Together, they collided.

Small exchanges behaved predictably. Larger shifts didn't. Momentum formed and dissolved quickly. A single comment reframed the room. A minor signal altered direction.

Plans still mattered. Intentions still mattered. But they no longer explained what happened next.

When independent thinkers gather, behavior stops being linear. Whether that room is a stadium, a feed, or a conference table.

Chapter 4

When Our Creations Get Away From Us

"People think they think upon the evidence. In fact they think on the basis of what makes them feel comfortable."

— *Bertrand Russell*

Some things begin as a whisper.

A joke.

A sarcastic comment.

A meme shared for fun.

Most days, that's all it is.

But somewhere between early social platforms and algorithmic everything, whispers stopped fading. They lingered. They multiplied. Sometimes they grew teeth.

In a world engineered for virality, the distance between harmless and harmful has collapsed. A joke becomes a movement. A rumor hardens into belief. A stray idea snowballs into a crowd convinced it has always known the truth.

Whether we notice it or not, whether we intend it or not.

Because the systems we use amplify whatever captures attention — not whatever deserves it.

Outrage Is Efficient

Algorithms don't have opinions. They have incentives.

Content that sparks emotion, laughter, fear, disgust, outrage, travels farther than anything nuanced. Calm explanations rarely spread. Certainty does. Simplicity does.

This is a feature.

The most extreme version of an idea often wins because extremity performs well. It grabs attention quickly and invites reaction. The system doesn't ask whether the idea is accurate. It asks whether it keeps people engaged.

Ideas once moved at the speed of conversation. Now they move at the speed of algorithms, amplified and recirculated before anyone pauses to question them.

From Echo to Avalanche

Repetition becomes reinforcement. Familiarity lowers skepticism. Emotion fills gaps logic would question. When enough people encounter the same idea, social pressure follows.

"People are talking about this" becomes "people believe this."

"People believe this" becomes "I probably should too."

"I believe this" becomes "This is just how things are."

The crowd feels present, even when it exists only in your feed.

The stadium shrank to the size of a phone, but the crowd feels larger than ever.

A version of this played out during the early days of the pandemic. Photos of empty grocery shelves began circulating. There wasn't an actual shortage at first. Repetition did its work.

People didn't panic because they needed supplies. They panicked because others appeared to believe they would. Momentum made the shortage real.

The Feedback Loop

Platforms don't merely reflect behavior. They accelerate it.

Outrage draws attention.

Attention triggers amplification.

Amplification creates normalization.

Normalization encourages action.

The system rewards what moves fastest. Once repetition builds belief and emotion drives reaction, momentum takes over.

This is how movements appear overnight.

How panic erupts from a headline.

How conspiracies outrun corrections.

How jokes harden into worldviews.

Not because people suddenly changed, but because the machinery rewards momentum, not meaning.

When Groups Stop Thinking

Give humans fear, familiarity, validation, and speed, and something predictable happens: individuals dissolve into a herd.

This isn't stupidity. It's biology. Humans evolved to read social cues quickly. When uncertainty rises, we look sideways instead of inward. We match tone. We move with the group because the group once meant safety.

The problem is scale.

When micro-behaviors amplify into macro-movements, influence stops being subtle. It becomes explosive.

We like to believe we control our creations. Often, they steer us.

The Consequence of Scale

When platforms began turning individual reactions into collective momentum, influence crossed a threshold.

What once required leadership and sustained effort can now emerge from a handful of emotionally charged posts.

Ideas no longer need to be correct to spread.

They only need to be contagious.

Systems don't ask whether a belief is stable or ethical. They ask whether it moves.

And movement doesn't drift toward truth. It drifts toward whatever is easiest to react to.

The Uncomfortable Pattern

These systems weren't built to manipulate, at least not explicitly. They were built to connect and optimize. But optimization without judgment produces momentum, not wisdom.

Momentum doesn't care where it's going.

And once you see this pattern, you realize that it shows up wherever humans gather.

Step Back for a Moment

The Pattern

Systems created to serve us can slowly begin to shape us, often drifting far from the intentions that created them.

Reflect on This

When do you react fastest to information?

What emotions accelerate your responses?

Pattern Interrupt: Wait Before You Share

The next time you feel the urge to forward, repost, or repeat a piece of information, wait thirty minutes.

Revisit the decision after the pause.

Notice how often urgency fades once time enters the equation.

Chapter 5

THE INFLUENCE YOU DIDN'T SEE

"We do not see things as they are, we see them as we are."

— Anaïs Nin

Walk into any meeting, family discussion, or project kickoff, and it's tempting to assume everyone is starting from the same place. The same facts. The same tone. The same understanding.

They aren't.

By the time people gather physical or virtual their minds have already been shaped by hours, days, sometimes years of invisible influence. The articles skimmed that morning. Assumptions reinforced by their feeds. The residue of unread emails, message pings, or a tense conversation earlier in the day. Their sleep. Their stress. Their last interaction with you.

You're not meeting people where you think they are.

You're meeting them where their minds already landed.

And the same is true for you.

Why the Same Room Holds Multiple Realities

The brain isn't a neutral recorder. It's a meaning-making machine. It filters, compresses, predicts, and fills gaps before conscious thought gets involved. That's why two people can sit through the same conversation and walk out describing entirely different events.

One thinks the decision was clear.

Another thinks it was avoided.

A third didn't realize a decision was being made.

This isn't incompetence. It's perception.

A classic example played out during the Bay of Pigs invasion, a failed U.S.-backed attempt in the early 1960s to overthrow Fidel Castro. Senior leaders heard the same briefings and walked away with different assumptions. Some believed the invasion would remain small and deniable. Others expected a popular uprising or military backup if things failed. Silence was mistaken for agreement. Agreement was mistaken for alignment. The result wasn't just a failed operation, it deepened Cold War tensions and set the stage for far more dangerous confrontations.

The stakes in your meetings may be lower. The mechanism is the same. Leaders say, "I was very clear." They were, in their own heads. Everyone else heard a version shaped by context, fear, status, and experience.

The Invisible Variables Everyone Brings

Teams never enter a room as blank slates. They arrive with mental tabs already open.

The engineer who hears feedback as criticism.

The product manager who skimmed a thread at dawn and now believes the project is behind.

The analyst who stays quiet because past ideas were dismissed.

The extrovert who fills silence because they process aloud.

None are wrong. None are seeing the same thing.

Alignment dissolves because people leave carrying different realities, each internally coherent, each incomplete.

Inside Every Conversation, Multiple Stories Run

Picture a leadership meeting. Someone frowns at a slide. Another assumes disagreement. A third senses tension and becomes defensive. A fourth assumes they're missing something and mentally rewrites their workload.

All from a single expression.

Perception gaps widen not because people intend dysfunction, but because the brain hates ambiguity and fills it with familiar stories. What's labeled "misalignment" is often disagreement about reality.

When people say, "We're not on the same page," they usually mean, "We were never reading the same book."

Once you see this, leadership shifts.

You stop assuming resistance and start noticing influence.

You stop pushing for agreement and start paying attention to meaning.

You stop reacting to behavior and start asking what story that behavior makes sense inside.

Awareness doesn't eliminate complexity.

But it gives you a chance to work with it instead of being surprised by it.

Quick Reflection

The Pattern

Influence rarely shows up as persuasion.

More often, it hides inside the environment, shaping behavior long before anyone realizes it is happening.

Reflect on This

Think about the last time your team adopted a new tool, process, or idea. Did people change because they were convinced, or because the environment made the new behavior easier?

In your organization, what systems quietly guide behavior? Incentives, dashboards, reporting structures, meeting norms?

Where might those systems be encouraging behavior that leaders never explicitly asked for?

Pattern Interrupt

Pick one routine in your team this week, a meeting format, a reporting process, or a decision rule.

Change a single element of the environment and watch what happens to people's behavior.

Sometimes the fastest way to influence people is not to persuade them, but to change the system they are operating inside.

Chapter 6

When the Herd Runs Wild

"Madness is rare in individuals—but in groups, parties, nations, and ages it is the rule."

— Friedrich Nietzsche

Humans like to believe we're rational, that when something dramatic happens, we'll assess the facts and decide thoughtfully. It's a comforting story. It's mostly fiction.

Individually, people are often reasonable. In groups, reason competes with something stronger: momentum. When emotion, uncertainty, and speed collide, the herd wakes up. Not the mildly disorganized kind. The stampede kind.

This isn't a failure of intelligence. It's human nature.

We don't become different people in crowds, we become amplified versions of ourselves. Anxiety becomes panic. A half-formed idea hardens into certainty. A misunderstanding gains weight because others seem to react. Herd behavior doesn't need logic. It needs motion.

How a Herd Starts Moving

A herd rarely erupts from nowhere. It begins when three conditions overlap.

First, emotion enters, fear, excitement, outrage, belonging. Emotion speeds decisions and short-circuits nuance.

Second, ambiguity. The facts are incomplete or contested.

Third, social proof. Someone reacts decisively, and others take that reaction as signal.

This pattern is ancient. If the group ran, you ran. The one who paused didn't survive. Our nervous systems still carry that logic, even if modern threats are abstract.

Today it doesn't take a predator. It takes a headline. A panicked message. A viral post. A spike of urgency in a meeting.

Once those conditions align, movement begins.

When Emotion Outruns Truth

History offers reminders.

In seventeenth-century Salem Massachusetts, a handful of accusations triggered escalating fear. Neighbors watched neighbors. Silence became suspicious. Questioning the narrative felt dangerous. Over time, the community stopped asking whether accusations were true and started asking why so many people would say them if they weren't. Fear plus repetition plus reinforcement created a reality few felt safe challenging, until innocent people were imprisoned, executed, and the community was torn apart.

Nothing about that moment required ignorance. It required momentum.

Centuries later, the NASA Challenger launch decision followed a similar pattern. Engineers raised concerns about the O-rings. The information existed. What failed wasn't intelligence, but group dynamics. As pressure mounted, dissent softened. Silence filled the room. No one wanted to halt progress. The cost was catastrophic. Seven astronauts lost their lives.

Herd behavior doesn't always look chaotic. Sometimes it looks like professionalism and alignment at all costs.

Inside the Avalanche

Shared belief becomes shared action.

During the dot-com bubble, investors weren't persuaded by fundamentals alone. They were persuaded by participation. When confidence appeared universal, skepticism felt outdated. Caution felt naive. By the time the bubble burst, many admitted they doubted the valuations they just didn't want to be the only one stepping off.

Once movement begins, stopping feels riskier than continuing.

More recently, digital movements, conspiracy communities, and meme-stock frenzies have spread less through airtight logic than through belonging. Participation outweighed accuracy. Questioning the narrative felt like betrayal. Opposition strengthened conviction.

The herd didn't just move.

It defended itself.

The Illusion of Consensus

Herd behavior easily creates the sense that "everyone" agrees.

A few loud voices represent the whole.

Emotional reactions become consensus.

Silence becomes alignment.

People assume that if something were truly wrong, someone else would say so — not realizing everyone is thinking the same thing.

This is how teams chase the wrong problem.

How leaders overcorrect to satisfy the loudest few.

How decisions feel obvious in the moment and baffling later.

Emotion plus repetition plus social proof doesn't produce truth. It produces perceived reality. And perceived reality drives action.

When the Herd Turns Inward

Herd behavior doesn't require millions of people. It appears wherever humans gather, in workplaces, families, and leadership teams.

One anxious person raises the room's temperature.

One confident voice sets direction.

One misunderstood email sparks urgency.

One leader's mood shapes the day.

We imagine herd behavior happens "out there." It happens constantly "in here."

The mechanics are simple:

emotion spreads,

ambiguity invites interpretation,

social cues guide behavior,

momentum replaces reflection.

No one decides to follow the herd. It feels easier, safer, faster than resisting.

Herd behavior isn't a moral failure.

It's a social one.

Humans aren't irrational, they're relational. When uncertainty rises, we look sideways for cues. When speed increases, we borrow confidence from the group. When stakes feel high, we outsource thinking to momentum.

Leaders who understand this stop being surprised by it. They notice contagion, emotional, cognitive, behavioral, and see when it begins to accelerate.

Because once the herd is running, steering becomes exponentially harder.

The herd will always exist.

The question is whether anyone notices when it starts to run.

Take a Breath

The Pattern

Groups amplify behavior. Once momentum builds inside a crowd, individuals often follow the direction of the herd rather than their own independent judgment.

Reflect on This

When have you gone along with a group decision simply because momentum was building?

When did you last question the pace of a discussion?

Pattern Interrupt: Slow the Momentum

During the next fast-moving discussion, ask one thoughtful question that slows the room.

It might be:

"What assumption are we making here?"

Notice how the tone of the conversation shifts when the pace changes.

SECTION 3
MANAGING YOURSELF IN THE MIDDLE OF THE NOISE

By now, it's tempting to locate the problem out there. The herd. The team. The crowd that panics, rushes, misreads, amplifies the wrong things.

It's comforting to believe that if you understand group dynamics well enough, you'll be immune to them.

You won't.

Every system we've discussed works because it works on everyone, including the people who can explain it. Seeing the pattern doesn't remove you from it. It only gives you a brief moment of choice before it pulls again.

Here's what most leadership books miss: before you misread a room, the room has already misread you.

Your stress leaks. Your assumptions travel. Your unexamined reactions set the tone faster than your words.

The most important work doesn't start with influencing others. It starts with noticing what all of this is doing to you.

Because once your internal signal distorts, everything downstream distorts with it.

Chapter 7

It's Time To Hit Reset

"Between stimulus and response there is a space.
In that space is our power to choose our response."
— *Viktor Frankl*

If you've been nodding along about algorithms, herds, misread rooms, and spirals there's probably been a quieter thought underneath it all:

Okay, but what about me?

It's easy to treat influence as external. The feed. The crowd. The system. It's harder to admit you feel it too that even when you don't follow the herd, your footing still shifts.

This is where the conversation usually turns to stress.

"I need to slow down."

"I'm doing too much."

"I just need to be calmer."

Slowing down helps. But that's not the real issue.

Most of us think we're operating at full capacity when we're nowhere close.

The Illusion of "I'm Functioning Fine"

People say:

"I'm busy, but I've got it."

"I'm juggling a lot, but I'm handling it."

What they often mean is: nothing has broken yet.

But functioning isn't the same as seeing clearly.

When your mind is overloaded, it doesn't fail dramatically. It keeps going slightly off. You misread tone. Miss signals. Fill gaps with assumptions. Make decisions that feel reasonable in the moment and confusing later.

You're still moving. Just a few degrees off course.

And a few degrees, sustained long enough, take you far from where you intended to go.

Why Noise Is More Dangerous Than Stress

The problem isn't difficulty. Humans handle hard.

The problem is the absence of space. No natural pause between inputs.

Messages, feeds, alerts, meetings, headlines. Even in quiet moments, your brain braces for the next interruption.

So you adapt.

You get used to the hum.

Silence feels strange.

Stillness feels unproductive.

Gradually, your accuracy drops.

Leadership, judgment, communication begin to wobble, not from incompetence, but from static.

That's when you hear:

"I don't know why that went sideways."

"I thought we were aligned."

"It made sense at the time."

It probably did, from inside the noise.

Resetting Isn't About Calm. It's About Clarity.

Resetting isn't about relaxation. It's about accuracy.

A cluttered mind misreads tone. Fills ambiguity with fear. Overreacts to weak signals and misses strong ones. Leading from that state is like driving through fog and assuming everyone else sees clearly.

History is full of intelligent leaders who lacked clarity. The Challenger launch decision is one example. The data existed. The warnings were voiced.

But stress, pressure, and group dynamics filtered what people were willing to hear.

Resetting, even briefly, doesn't soften you. It sharpens you.

A calm but overloaded mind still misjudges. A calm but half-present leader still misses what's happening in the room.

Resetting restores signal.

When noise drops, perception improves. You hear what's said, and what isn't. You stop reacting to what's loud and start noticing what matters.

That isn't self-care. It's decision hygiene.

What Resetting Actually Fixes

A real reset doesn't make life easier. It makes perception cleaner.

It lets your brain close a few tabs.
It brings focus back into alignment.
Reduces small, avoidable errors that compound.

You don't move slower.
You waste less motion.

And if you lead others, that matters.

Your misreads ripple outward.

Why Resetting Is So Hard

Modern systems are excellent at manufacturing urgency. Every notification suggests something important might be waiting. Usually it isn't. But your brain checks anyway.

We call it multitasking. It's constant context switching. And every switch leaves residue, attention that never fully returns.

After a while, you're nowhere completely.

That's when people feel slightly on edge. Not burned out. Just... off.

Reset Doesn't Mean Disappearing

This isn't about deleting apps or pretending the modern world doesn't exist.

It's about interrupting momentum long enough to regain authorship over your attention.

Sometimes it's small:

- Fewer notifications
- Less background noise
- Intentional pauses where nothing new comes in

Sometimes it's simply remembering what it feels like to do one thing at a time.

That's enough to recalibrate.

The world won't slow down. Systems will keep optimizing for speed and engagement. Influence will keep getting quieter and more precise.

If you don't reset, you don't just get tired you get inaccurate.

And inaccurate leaders rarely fail dramatically. They drift. They misjudge. They make decisions that seem logical and unravel in practice.

Resetting isn't stepping away from responsibility.

It's how you remain capable of it.

You don't need to stop moving.

You just need to pause long enough to make sure you're still steering.

A Moment of Awareness

The Pattern

Real change rarely begins with new tools or strategies. It begins when people pause long enough to question the patterns they have been following automatically.

Reflect on This

When do you make decisions while mentally overloaded?

What role does noise play in your thinking?

Pattern Interrupt: Create Silence

Block twenty uninterrupted minutes this week. No messages, notifications, or inputs.

Use the time to think about one unresolved question.

Notice how differently problems look once the noise disappears.

Chapter 8

It Hurts, But It's Worth It

"What we resist persists."

— Carl Jung

Change has terrible timing.

It rarely arrives when you're rested and generous with your energy. It shows up when you're stretched, tired, already thinking, Can we not add one more thing?

And yet, the moments that shift your life, not cosmetically but fundamentally, share one trait:

They're uncomfortable.

Not cinematic suffering. Just enough friction to make you question if it's worth it. Growth rarely feels noble while it's happening. It feels irritating. Slightly painful. Sometimes exhausting.

Which is why so many people avoid it. Not consciously, but strategically. Doing nothing becomes a perfectly rational strategy.

Why Discomfort Is the Price of Entry

We've trained ourselves to expect progress without strain. One-click solutions. Effortless optimization. Results without resistance.

Meaningful change has never worked that way.

It's closer to returning to the gym after a long break. The weights feel heavier than you remember. Your body argues for starting tomorrow. Nothing about the first session feels good, except realizing the next day that you didn't break. You adapted.

The discomfort wasn't punishment.

It was the cost of admission.

The Two Pains Nobody Mentions

Pain shows up either way. The only choice is which version you'll face.

There's the pain of discipline, short-lived and irritating. Turning off notifications. Staying focused past comfort. Choosing effort over escape. It stings, then fades.

And there's the pain of regret, slow and compounding. Realizing you stayed comfortable instead of curious. Distracted instead of deliberate. Safe instead of growing.

One pain ends.

The other accumulates interest.

Most people don't avoid discomfort. They postpone it.

Why Discomfort Works (Even When Your Brain Objects)

Your brain isn't built for growth. It's built for survival. Survival logic treats unfamiliar effort as risk, even when it benefits you.

That's why beginnings feel awkward. Why learning feels clumsy. Why the right move often feels worse than the easy one.

But the brain adapts quickly.

Each time you stay in discomfort slightly longer than your instincts prefer, the next attempt costs less. What felt impossible becomes manageable. What felt awkward becomes automatic.

That shift isn't motivation.

It's conditioning.

Progress Has Always Been Inconvenient

The Wright brothers didn't drift into flight comfortably. Their early attempts resembled crashes.

Marie Curie worked in conditions that would close modern labs, under-resourced and physically taxing, because discovery required it.

Thomas Edison reframed repeated failures as information. Failure wasn't the detour. It was the method.

Michelangelo painted the Sistine Chapel twisted into positions no one would recommend. Comfort was irrelevant to the vision.

Nelson Mandela spent 27 years imprisoned and emerged clearer, not smaller.

Across centuries, the pattern repeats:

Most move toward ease.

A few move toward discomfort.

Progress follows the few.

Comfort preserves.

Discomfort creates.

The Trap of Modern Convenience

Today, ease is marketed as wisdom. Don't cook, click. Don't think, scroll. Don't struggle, distract.

Convenience feels helpful in the moment. Over time, it erodes the muscles required to begin, persist, and finish.

When everything is easy, effort feels unnecessary.

When effort feels unnecessary, growth feels optional.
When growth feels optional, potential remains theoretical.

Convenience doesn't ruin us loudly.
It does it politely.

Micro-Discomfort Beats Reinvention

Discomfort rarely requires dramatic overhaul. It starts small.

Twenty-five focused minutes instead of endless switching.
Starting for five minutes instead of waiting for motivation.
Doing the uncomfortable task before the urgent one.

These aren't productivity tricks. They're negotiations with a brain wired for comfort.

Each time you resist distraction, you strengthen focus.
Each time you stay with discomfort, you expand capacity.
Each time you finish what once intimidated you, you reinforce something quieter than confidence:

This is survivable.

That belief compounds not as ego, but as capacity.

Discomfort doesn't arrive looking useful. It shows up as inconvenience, resistance, irritation. But nearly every meaningful shift asks the same question:

Will you stay, or retreat to what's familiar?

Most of the time, the answer shapes less what you do and more what you're willing to tolerate.

Pause and Consider

The Pattern

Growth often requires discomfort because breaking existing mental patterns challenges the identity and beliefs we have grown comfortable with.

Reflect on This

What difficult task have you been postponing?

What uncomfortable conversation is waiting to happen?

Pattern Interrupt: Do the Hard Thing First

Tomorrow morning, begin the day with the task you've been avoiding.

Notice whether the discomfort was greater before you started or while you were doing it.

Chapter 9

WHAT ARE YOU TELLING YOURSELF?

"The greatest trick the mind ever played was convincing us it was telling the truth."

— *Anonymous*

Most of us move through our days accompanied by a voice we barely notice. It narrates while we work, decide, react, hesitate, occasionally spiral. It comments on what we did well, what we messed up, what this means about us, what's likely to happen next. We treat it like background noise sometimes annoying, occasionally useful, mostly harmless.

It isn't.

That voice isn't just narrating your life.

It's shaping it.

Every belief you hold about yourself your competence, limits, confidence, agency is built from stories you repeat internally. The most influential story you'll ever hear won't come from a boss, book, or parent. It comes from you, on a loop, usually unchallenged.

So the question is simple and uncomfortable:

What story are you telling yourself especially when things don't go as planned?

The Architecture of Self-Talk

Self-talk is the architecture of identity. Each thought is a brick. Repetition hardens into structure.

When you tell yourself, *I'm not good at this*, you aren't stating a fact you're building a room and convincing yourself there's no door.

When you tell yourself, *I'll figure this out*, you're not guaranteeing success, but you're keeping exits visible.

Self-talk becomes the lens for everything else. The same feedback can feel like attack or data. The same delay can feel like failure or information. The same challenge, a threat or a puzzle.

Elite athletes understand this. Sports psychology doesn't just train bodies; it trains dialogue. Under pressure, negative self-talk tightens muscles, narrows attention, accelerates mistakes. Productive self-talk steadies, widens perspective, keeps people in the game.

Your mind listens to your voice, even when it's silent.

Repetition Writes the Script

Few of these stories started with you. A teacher dismissed an idea. A manager made an offhand comment. A parent tried to help and missed. A classmate laughed at the wrong moment. None decisive alone. Repeated internally, they became familiar.

And familiarity disguises itself as truth.

Repetition doesn't require accuracy, only consistency. If an external algorithm can shape belief through exposure, imagine what your internal one can do when it runs for years unchecked.

Most self-talk isn't fact.

It's accumulated commentary hardened into certainty.

How Self-Talk Shapes Action

History makes this visible.

Nelson Mandela spent twenty-seven years imprisoned in an environment full of material for bitterness or defeat. Either narrative would have been understandable. Either could have consumed him. Instead, he framed his experience through dignity and long-term purpose. "I never lose. I either win or learn." That wasn't optimism. It was survival architecture. The story preserved his capacity to lead when the moment arrived.

During the Apollo 13 mission, an oxygen tank exploded mid-mission. The situation was dire: failing systems, limited power, no margin for error. Panic would have been reasonable. Fatalism easy. Instead, astronauts and ground crew anchored to a disciplined narrative: *This is a problem. Problems can be solved.*

That framing didn't erase risk. It shaped behavior. Attention stayed on options, not fear. The mission failed. The crew lived.

Your inner narrative doesn't describe reality.

It determines what actions feel available.

When the story is *I'm stuck*, you stop scanning for exits.

When it's *This is impossible*, creativity collapses.

When it's *I can learn my way through this*, behavior follows.

Change the story and you don't magically change reality but you change how you move inside it. Over time, that difference compounds.

The Algorithm in Your Head

Your internal voice is constantly fed by external inputs: feeds, curated success stories, productivity myths, outrage cycles, comparison disguised as inspiration. Scroll long enough and the whisper shifts: *You're behind.*

Spend time where effort is normalized, and the tone begins to change.

The external algorithm curates content.
The internal one curates identity.

Neither is neutral.

Reclaiming the Narrative

You can't rewrite a story you haven't heard. The first step isn't affirmation. It's attention.

Notice what your mind says when you fail, succeed unexpectedly, try something new. Listen to the tone. Instructional or punitive? Curious or dismissive?

Often, the voice is repeating lines you didn't write. Once you hear the line, you can question it:

When did I start believing this?

Who handed me this story?

Is there evidence or just repetition?

Make edits, not grand rewrites.

Not *I'll never figure this out*, but *I haven't yet.*

Not *I'm not good enough*, but *I'm learning.*

That isn't self-deception. It's authorship.

Your life is a narrative in progress. You are both protagonist and writer, whether you acknowledge it or not. Every belief becomes a scene. Every assumption, a plotline. Every repeated thought nudges the story forward.

Over time, repetition starts to feel like truth.

The stories we tell ourselves don't feel like influence.

But they shape the lives we end up living.

Look Inward

The Pattern

The stories we tell ourselves shape our actions far more than the facts we encounter.

Reflect on This

What story appears in your mind when things go wrong?

Who might have influenced that narrative earlier in your life?

Pattern Interrupt: Rewrite the Sentence

The next time you catch yourself thinking something discouraging about your abilities, rewrite the sentence in more accurate language.

Not more positive. Just more precise.

Notice whether the new framing changes your next action.

Chapter 10

You're Saying It, But Do You Mean It?

"The beginning of wisdom is the definition of terms."

— Socrates

Words are easy. We say them constantly: *I value authenticity. I practice mindfulness. I prioritize self-care. I'm living my purpose.*

But there's a harder question underneath those statements:

If your actions were examined, would they confirm your words?

We live in a culture fluent in meaningful language. Catchphrases and values circulate widely, making it easy to sound reflective while living on autopilot. The problem isn't the words themselves. It's the confusion between naming a value and embodying it.

When language is repeated without practice, it loses force.

When Words Drift

Meaning rarely disappears all at once. It thins through repetition without intention.

Authenticity once required living in alignment with your truth, even when it cost approval. Now it is often reduced to curated self-expression labeled "real." The word remains; the risk fades.

Self-care began as preservation, choosing yourself in environments that drained you. Today, it's often shorthand for comfort or avoidance. Not inherently wrong, but narrower than it once was.

Mindfulness, rooted in disciplined awareness, is often reframed as a productivity tool. Presence, instead of being an end in itself, becomes a performance enhancer.

This shift isn't malicious. It's gradual. When ideas are repeated casually or commercialized, their depth flattens.

Why Meaning Erodes

Words weaken when they are:

Used more than examined
Claimed more than practiced
Shared more than understood

Eventually, signaling replaces substance. We talk about values more than we measure ourselves against them.

The change is subtle but consequential. Behavior adapts to match the diluted meaning.

When Ideals Lose Their Center

The same pattern appears beyond personal language.

The American Dream began as a belief in dignity and opportunity. Over time, it narrowed into a checklist of possessions. The phrase stayed powerful. The meaning shifted.

When definitions change, actions follow.

The surface remains. The center moves.

The Cost of Saying Without Doing

When strong language is used casually, it creates emotional inflation. Everything sounds important. Nothing feels anchored.

Self-awareness turns into performance. Growth becomes labeling. Alignment becomes branding.

The issue is not the vocabulary. Authenticity, mindfulness, and self-care still matter.

But they regain weight only when they shape behavior.

If you value authenticity, where are you willing to risk approval?

If you practice mindfulness, where are you choosing presence over distraction?

If you prioritize self-care, what are you protecting?

A word becomes real the moment it costs something.

Until then, it is only language.

One More Check

The Pattern

Communication fails when leaders assume clarity while others interpret messages through their own experiences and assumptions.

Reflect on This

Which values do you say matter most to you?

Where might your behavior quietly contradict them?

Pattern Interrupt: Make the Value Visible

Choose one value you believe in and demonstrate it through one visible action this week.

It might be giving credit publicly, listening longer than usual, or speaking up when something feels off.

Notice how small actions reinforce what you claim to believe.

SECTION 4
LEADING WHEN NO ONE HAS TO FOLLOW YOU

Because leading anyone else starts with leading the only mind you fully control, your own. So far, the lens has been inward.

We've examined how systems shape belief, how groups amplify momentum, and how judgment slips when speed and noise take over. You've seen how thinking drifts, how stories form, and how accuracy erodes long before anything visibly breaks.

Now comes the harder part: none of it stays contained.

You are not outside the system. You are inside it, and so is everyone responding to you. Your reactions travel. Your assumptions set the tone. Your urgency becomes someone else's pressure.

This is where leadership begins, whether you asked for it or not.

The moment others adjust their behavior in response to yours, you're no longer only managing yourself. You're shaping the environment.

What follows is about that shift, when influence is subtle, authority is optional, and people align not because they're required to, but because the environment makes it reasonable.

This isn't work that comes after leadership.
It's what makes leadership visible.

Chapter 11

THEY'RE LISTENING, BUT ARE THEY HEARING?

"Every system is perfectly designed to get the results it gets."

— W. Edwards Deming

Managing people is less like giving instructions and more like speaking into moving air. You explain something. Heads nod. Someone smiles. It feels settled. Then an hour later, the message has shifted or vanished entirely.

This is one of leadership's most persistent illusions: that hearing equals understanding.

Anyone who has led a team, taught a class, given feedback, raised children, or sent an email knows the truth. Listening is common. Hearing is rare.

What makes this harder is that the problem isn't just them. You've missed cues. Misread tone. Filled in gaps with assumptions that felt reasonable. Communication is mutual and so is misunderstanding. Most breakdowns aren't driven by bad intent. They're driven by the belief that we were clear when we were only audible.

Leadership isn't broadcasting information. It's the discipline of mutual hearing. Without that, you're not leading. You're speaking and hoping alignment happens.

Humans Have Always Struggled to Hear

It's easy to blame technology, but humans were mishearing each other long before email and notifications.

Ancient Greek assemblies, often praised as early democracy, were loud, theatrical, and swayed by performance. Aristotle noted that people responded to rhetoric more than substance. Volume and persuasion were mistaken for clarity and understanding. In that environment, rhetoric didn't just emerge as an art, it became a core competency. If you wanted to be heard, you had to be persuasive, not necessarily precise.

We haven't changed as much as we think. We've just improved the amplification.

The Illusion of Connection

Modern tools promised connection. They delivered access.

We exchange more messages and attend more meetings than any generation before us. But connection without comprehension is noise.

Information moves faster than anyone can process. Meaning falls behind.

When someone says, "Got it," what they often mean is, "I think I understand." Under overload, attention fragments. Messages compete. Nuance disappears.

The problem isn't indifference. It's saturation.

When Leaders Don't Hear

The consequences sharpen when leaders fail to receive what's being said around them.

After the Deepwater Horizon oil spill, one of the worst environmental disasters in U.S. history, BP executives communicated constantly as the crisis dragged on for weeks. Statements were issued. Briefings were held. But more than a month into the disaster, while the well was still leaking and Gulf communities were still living with the damage, the CEO publicly said, "I'd like my life back." The remark landed as a striking example of tone-deaf leadership, a leader speaking from personal frustration while others were still living through grief, fear, and loss. He had spoken. He had not heard what the moment required.

In that moment, public perception shifted. The gap between what was said and what was felt became impossible to ignore.

They were communicating. They were not connecting.

When people feel unheard, trust erodes. When trust erodes, followership collapses.

Leadership has never depended on how clearly you speak. It depends on how accurately you receive meaning.

Why Hearing Breaks Down

Several forces interfere with real listening:

- Confirmation bias filters what fits our existing views.
- Mental rehearsing pulls attention toward our response instead of their message.
- Cognitive overload fragments focus.

The result is predictable: two people leave the same conversation both feeling unheard.

Often, neither intended harm. They were each navigating internal noise.

The Cost of Missing Each Other

When hearing fails, consequences accumulate. Teams grow tense. Departments silo. Relationships repeat unresolved arguments. Communities polarize.

In extreme cases, organizations collapse. At Enron, warning signs about unethical accounting and internal risk were present long before the company imploded. Leadership did not want to hear them. What began as selective deafness hardened into culture, and culture became collapse.

Ignoring signals is costly.

Hearing selectively is costly.

Failing to hear at all is usually the most expensive mistake in the room.

Leadership is not built on how well you speak.

It is built on how well you receive meaning.

Before You Turn the Page

The Pattern

Communication fails when leaders assume clarity while others interpret messages through their own experiences and assumptions.

Reflect on This

When you explain something important, how do you know people understood it the same way you meant it?

Where might alignment be assumed rather than confirmed?

What signals tell you that a message has actually landed?

Pattern Interrupt: The Takeaway Test

At the end of your next meeting or discussion, ask one simple question:

"What is everyone taking away from this conversation?"

Listen to the answers without correcting them immediately.

Notice how similar or different the interpretations are. Alignment often looks clearer from the front of the room than it does from the seats.

Chapter 12

LEADING AMONG CATS

"If you want to go fast, go alone. If you want to go far, go together."
— African proverb

When a team is small, alignment happens naturally. Conversations circulate. Decisions move quickly. Everyone sees roughly the same thing at the same time.

Add more people more expertise, more perspectives, more motivations — and the dynamic changes. The group stops behaving like a single organism and starts resembling a room full of cats. Brilliant. Capable. Each convinced their beam of light matters most.

This is where leadership shifts. It stops being coordination and becomes orchestration.

You can't corral adults. What works consistently is purpose. Not the decorative kind. The kind clear and compelling enough that independent minds choose to move in the same direction.

When purpose is sharp, people run toward it.

When it's vague or transactional, they don't rebel. They drift.

The Complexity of Large Groups

As groups grow, strain increases.

Communication thins. Perspectives multiply. Accountability diffuses until work drifts into "I assumed someone else was handling it."

In small teams, cohesion is proximity.

In large teams, cohesion is constructed.

This is where purpose functions as gravity. It keeps difference from becoming noise.

Without it, you don't get diversity of thought. You get chaos with opinions.

When Herding Cats Works

The Manhattan Project, the secret U.S.-led wartime effort that brought together scientists to develop the atomic bomb, should have failed. The team was filled with towering intellects, clashing egos, and constant disagreement.

Yet they moved together. The urgency was larger than the weapon itself. Many believed that if the Nazis gained that kind of power first, the world would fall under something far darker. Purpose didn't remove conflict, but it gave it direction.

NASA's Apollo program followed the same pattern. Engineers, mathematicians, pilots, and visionaries would never naturally synchronize.

Then they were given a target.

A deadline.

A reason.

Point at the moon with conviction, and complexity organizes itself.

Purpose didn't tame disagreement. It directed it.

When the Herd Scatters

NASA also offers the counterpoint.

Before the Challenger launch, engineers raised concerns about the O-rings.

The warnings existed. They did not travel far enough to interrupt schedule pressure and momentum. In that moment, schedule had become louder than purpose.

Purpose is clearest at the beginning. When something is new, urgency is sharp, attention is high, and challenge feels necessary. Over time, as repetition sets in, that edge softens. What once felt critical starts to feel routine.

When purpose weakens, people don't become reckless. They become quiet.

And in complex systems, silence is dangerous.

The Bay of Pigs unfolded similarly. Intelligent people sat at the table. But clarity had blurred into politics and fear. As the mission lost coherence, dissent softened. People complied.

Not because they agreed.

Because the purpose no longer compelled challenge.

That's when the cats scatter not in defiance, but in disconnection.

It's Not "Cats or No Cats"

The real question is: what are we trying to do?

If the work is routine and precision matters most, you need steadiness and reliability.

If the terrain is uncertain if you're innovating or attempting something ambitious you need the cats. The contrarians. The people comfortable with friction.

Purpose tells you which you need. It matches mission to mindset.

Purpose Is the Compass

Purpose aligns independent thinkers without flattening them.

It keeps scale from becoming noise.

It tells leaders when to tighten structure and when to release control.

Without purpose, you're herding cats in the dark.

With purpose, you're conducting something complex, unpredictable, and sometimes extraordinary.

Pause for a Moment

The Pattern

Independent thinkers bring creativity and insight, but leading them requires influence, trust, and shared purpose rather than control.

Reflect on This

Is your team aligned on what matters most right now?

Where might activity be replacing clarity?

How confident are you that everyone sees the same destination?

Pattern Interrupt: The One-Sentence Priority

Ask each member of your team to write down the organization's top priority in one sentence.

Collect the answers before discussing them.

Notice whether the responses point in the same direction or reveal multiple versions of the goal.

Chapter 13

Building Movements, Not Mandates

"People do not resist change. They resist being changed."

— Peter Senge

Influencing one person is difficult. Influencing hundreds or thousands is different entirely. Once you step beyond one-on-one conversations, your message must move through distraction, skepticism, and cognitive overload.

You're no longer just speaking. You're competing with inboxes, notifications, stress, and fatigue.

Which leads to the harder question: not how do you make them listen, but how do you make them care?

Not because you said it.

Because it matters to them.

Why People Don't Care (Yet)

Most people aren't indifferent. They're saturated.

Alerts, deadlines, obligations, and global noise fill their attention. Even important messages arrive as one more demand. When something feels abstract or overly polished, people don't argue. They disengage.

This isn't personal. It's the cost of attention scarcity.

Speaking louder doesn't solve it. Repeating yourself doesn't solve it. Relevance does.

Resonance cuts through because it feels human and specific.

Close the Distance

Influence doesn't work at a distance. It works inside conversation.

Franklin D. Roosevelt's Fireside Chats during the Great Depression weren't lectures. They felt like someone speaking directly into people's living rooms, steady explanations delivered in a tone that reduced panic and distance. He didn't inflate authority. He made it accessible.

Trust forms when leaders feel reachable.

Not impressive. Reachable.

What Makes People Care

People don't move because something is labeled important. They move when it becomes personal and actionable.

They care when the stakes are visible when they can see how something affects their lives, not just an abstract mission. Vague ideals rarely mobilize behavior. Tangible consequences do.

Stories translate complexity into experience. Malala Yousafzai's influence didn't come from secondhand accounts. It came from hearing her in her own words, a girl denied education, attacked for it, and still refusing to be silent. It came from lived truth that made injustice concrete.

And even when people care, they stall if action feels overwhelming. Momentum begins with steps that feel possible now. Small actions enable larger commitments.

Shared Identity

Caring accelerates when it becomes collective.

The American Civil Rights Movement endured not just through speeches, but through shared identity, language, symbols, rituals, belonging. People didn't simply support a cause. They became part of it.

When participation becomes identity, momentum sustains itself. It's no longer something you do occasionally. It becomes part of who you are, something you carry, defend, and act on even when it's difficult.

Where Influence Breaks

Influence erodes quietly.

It weakens when information increases but meaning decreases.

When outcomes are oversold.

When messages feel scripted instead of human.

When leaders speak at people instead of with them.

The strongest communicators stay grounded and specific. They choose clarity over performance.

Alignment Over Performance

People don't expect perfection. They expect consistency.

Patagonia, an outdoor clothing company known for its environmental stance builds loyalty because its actions reflect its stated values, from encouraging repair over replacement to taking public stands on environmental issues. Decisions reinforce promises. Authenticity isn't dramatic. It's repeated alignment.

Consistency builds trust. Trust sustains attention.

When Caring Spreads

When people genuinely care, influence no longer depends on your voice alone.

The ALS Ice Bucket Challenge spread because it was simple, visible, communal, and emotionally engaging. Participation became contagious.

That's how movements grow.

Not through mandates.

Through shared momentum.

STEP BACK FOR A SECOND

The Pattern

People rarely commit deeply to mandates. They commit to ideas that feel meaningful and shared.

Reflect on This

When do people follow because they must, versus because they believe?

What makes someone personally invested in a goal?

Pattern Interrupt: Lead With the Why

In your next conversation about an initiative, begin with the reason the work matters instead of the instructions for doing it.

Tell a short story about who the work affects or why it exists.

Notice how the energy of the discussion changes when meaning appears before direction.

Chapter 14

PEOPLE PROGRAMS, NOT HR POLICIES

"The best way to predict the future is to create it."

— Peter Drucker

There's a familiar sound inside companies: the quiet arrival of a new HR policy in someone's inbox. It's opened, skimmed, and forgotten. Work continues unchanged because nothing meaningful shifted.

A policy isn't a movement. It's documentation.

Policies are written to signal care.

Programs are built to demonstrate it.

Policies live in files. Programs live in behavior. And people recognize the difference immediately. They can feel the gap between what's declared and what's practiced.

You can write "we value respect" across walls and slide decks. But if people hesitate to speak because they expect dismissal or penalty, the message teaches the opposite lesson. Culture isn't what's announced. It's what people feel safe enough to attempt on an ordinary afternoon.

I once saw a company unveil a 74-page leadership framework, polished, beautifully branded. It was shared once. Then it disappeared.

Culture doesn't live in documents. It lives in daily behavior, especially when it's inconvenient.

Culture Isn't an HR Function

Organizations often assume HR owns culture. If that were true, culture would be consistent because HR usually cares deeply.

But HR cannot override a manager who shuts down ideas, a leader who praises innovation but punishes mistakes, or an executive team that speaks of transparency while withholding decisions.

Culture reflects experience, not intention.

Designing Identity, Not Rules

Most companies start culture with a policy. Walt Disney started with identity.

Employees weren't told simply to be friendly. They were Cast Members, stepping onto a stage when guests entered. The metaphor shaped behavior. It framed ordinary actions as part of a story.

Rules didn't make Disneyland feel consistent. Ritual and identity did.

That's the difference. A people program doesn't mandate behavior. It makes behavior meaningful.

When Nothing Changes

I watched another company launch "Culture 2.0" with banners,

workshops, and hype videos. Two months later, it was forgotten.

Employees didn't resist it. Daily incentives, promotions, and meeting dynamics simply stayed the same.

They issued messaging. They didn't redesign behavior.

A policy hopes people comply.

A program adjusts the environment so the right behavior becomes natural.

Designing the Room

Pixar didn't publish a policy about candor. They built the Braintrust.

Directors present unfinished films to peers. Everyone offers feedback. No one outranks the conversation. The director must hear the critique, but isn't obligated to follow it.

This wasn't a statement of values. It was structure. Candor became routine because the room demanded it.

Behavior wasn't heroic. It was expected.

That's what structure does. It turns values into habits.

Staging the Experience

When Airbnb introduced "Belong Anywhere," it wasn't just a tagline. New hires spent their first week living in an Airbnb with colleagues, experiencing what belonging felt like.

No memo can replicate that. No policy can create that imprint.

They didn't explain the value. They staged it.

The Real Difference

Policies tell people what the company wants.

Programs invite people into what the company is building.

Policies enforce.

Programs embed.

Policies ask for compliance.

Programs create ownership.

People rarely commit to what they're told to memorize.

They commit to what they help bring to life.

LOOK A LITTLE CLOSER

The Pattern

Policies may shape structure, but behavior changes when systems encourage participation, ownership, and human connection.

Reflect on This

What behaviors actually receive recognition in your organization?

What do people learn about culture by watching leaders interact?

Pattern Interrupt: The Recognition Audit

Over the next week, pay attention to moments when someone receives praise, visibility, or recognition.

Write down three examples.

Then compare those moments with the values your organization says it stands for.

Notice whether the behaviors being reinforced match the values being declared.

Section 5
What Big Tech Knows That You Can Use

If leadership were only about charisma or communication, this book could end here.

But something more consistent has been shaping outcomes for years often more reliably than any individual leader.

Systems.

Not abstract theory. Designed systems. The kind that determine what's easy, what's visible, what repeats, and what fades. They don't need authority. They don't argue. They simply make certain behaviors frictionless and others difficult.

This is where Big Tech enters the picture.

Not as a villain. As a disciplined student of human behavior.

While leaders debated motivation, platforms studied friction.

While organizations wrote values, products engineered defaults.

While managers tried to persuade, systems made action automatic.

If you want to understand modern influence, you have to understand how behavior is designed at scale.

Because whether you intend it or not, your teams are already operating inside these mechanics.

Chapter 15

THE MECHANICS OF MEANINGFUL INFLUENCE

"We shape our tools, and thereafter our tools shape us."

— Marshall McLuhan

Influence isn't magic. It isn't charisma. It's mechanics.

What Big Tech understands and many leaders still overlook is that behavior rarely changes because people are persuaded. It changes because environments, systems, and products are designed to guide action.

This chapter isn't about headlines or alarm. It's about how products are designed at scale, the behavioral science behind those decisions, and the choices made long before anything appears on a screen.

The First Design Question: Where Will People Drop Off?

When product teams design something new, they don't begin with, *How do we convince people?*

They ask:

- Where will people hesitate?

- Where will they get stuck?
- Where will effort exceed motivation?

Behavioral science shows that humans are highly sensitive to friction — extra steps, confusion, cognitive load, emotional risk. The moment something feels effortful or unclear, disengagement becomes the default.

Amazon's one-click purchase illustrates this clearly. The company didn't persuade customers to buy more. It simply removed checkout friction. Fewer steps meant fewer abandoned carts. When effort decreases, completion increases.

Not persuasion. Behavioral design.

Motivation Is Unreliable. Design Isn't.

Behavioral scientist BJ Fogg summarized behavior with a simple formula:

Behavior = Motivation × Ability × Prompt

Motivation fluctuates. Ability can be engineered.

Rather than hoping people feel inspired, product teams reduce effort so action feels easy even when motivation is low.

Netflix's autoplay feature removed the fragile pause between episodes. The company didn't increase desire; it eliminated the decision point. When friction disappears, behavior continues.

You see the same principle in:

- Default calendar invites
- Auto-renew subscriptions
- Saved preferences

Design absorbs effort.

Defaults Are Quietly Powerful

One of the strongest behavioral levers is the default. People tend to stick with what's pre-selected not necessarily because they agree, but because changing it requires effort.

Organ donation systems make this visible. Countries using opt-out policies see dramatically higher participation rates than opt-in countries. The difference isn't altruism. It's default design.

Tech platforms apply this constantly:

- Default notifications
- Default privacy settings
- Default feed ordering

Defaults don't remove choice.

They shape the path of least resistance.

Humans Learn by Watching

People rarely change behavior because they're told to. They change because they see others doing it.

When TikTok launched, users weren't greeted with instructions. They were shown examples trends, formats, sounds. Participation became learnable through observation. Visibility normalized action.

This principle appears in:

- Public activity feeds
- Contribution counters
- Shared dashboards

When behavior is visible, participation rises.

Social Proof Beats Logic

Humans look sideways before they move forward.

LinkedIn's profile completion bar didn't rely on persuasion. It showed progress and implied that others had finished. Completion felt normal. Stopping early felt incomplete.

Belonging drives behavior more reliably than instruction.

Feedback Loops Sustain Action

Behavior fades without feedback. Immediate signals tell us: *This matters. You're progressing.*

Duolingo didn't make language learning effortless. It made progress visible — streaks, reminders, gentle loss aversion.

The streak isn't the goal.

Consistency is.

Feedback creates momentum. Momentum sustains behavior.

Repetition Builds Identity

Product teams don't design for one-time action. They design for repetition.

Small actions, repeated, become habits.

Habits, sustained, become identity.

"I use this."

"I check this."

"This is what I do."

That isn't persuasion.

It's pattern formation.

Where Ethics Enter

These mechanics are powerful. That makes the intent of those designing them critical.

Ethical design:

- Makes beneficial behavior easier
- Clarifies consequences
- Preserves real choice
- Avoids hidden harm

The same tools that capture attention can support learning, health, connection, and safety.

The difference isn't knowledge.

It's responsibility.

Big Tech didn't master humans. It studied behavior.

Once you see the mechanics, influence stops looking mysterious.

It starts looking designed.

A Systems Check

The Pattern

Sustainable influence comes from shaping environments and incentives, not from forcing compliance.

Reflect on This

What behaviors does your organization's structure make easiest?

Where does doing the "right" thing require extra effort?

Pattern Interrupt: Walk the System

Choose one everyday process in your organization such as approving work, escalating a problem, or sharing ideas.

Follow the process step by step.

Notice what behavior the design of the system naturally encourages.

Systems rarely need instructions to influence behavior. Their structure does it quietly.

Chapter 16

How To Make People Care

"People will forget what you said, people will forget what you did, but people will never forget how you made them feel."

— Maya Angelou

Mechanics can start behavior.

They reduce friction. They remove obstacles. They make the first step easy.

But mechanics alone cannot sustain anything.

People might click once because it's simple.

They stay and bring others because it means something.

This is where many initiatives quietly fail. The design is clean. The rollout is smooth. The adoption graph rises for six weeks.

And then it stalls.

Because ease creates participation.

Meaning creates commitment.

The Myth of Apathy

When leaders ask, "Why don't people care?" what they often mean is, "Why don't people care about what I care about?"

Apathy is the easiest explanation.

It's almost always wrong.

Most people care deeply. Their care is simply already invested in their team's reputation, their manager's trust, their sense of competence, their future opportunities.

New initiatives aren't competing with laziness.

They're competing with priorities that already feel personal.

When a message doesn't connect to daily reality, momentum fades not because people resist, but because it never felt relevant.

Authority Gets Attention. Meaning Keeps It.

Authority can command attention.

Meaning earns it.

A senior leader announces a 'top priority.' Heads nod. Behavior stays the same.

Contrast that with what happens after something breaks publicly or hits close to home. Teams rally not because they were told to, but because it suddenly matters.

I've seen product teams adopt rigorous quality processes overnight after one painful release forced them to spend a weekend managing angry customers. The process stopped being about compliance.

It became about pride.

Authority starts conversations.

Meaning sustains them.

The Quiet Questions People Ask

Before investing effort, people run an internal filter:

- Does this tangibly affect my work or life?
- Do people like me take this seriously?
- Does participating say something about who I am?

If those answers are unclear, compliance might happen.

Caring won't.

That's why initiatives can look successful in reports but hollow in practice. People did what was required. They just never internalized why it mattered.

Stakes Beat Abstractions

Abstract goals rarely move people.

Concrete consequences do.

Saying, "We're improving documentation quality" generates little energy. Showing how poor documentation leads to midnight pages, stalled onboarding, and repetitive questions makes the issue human.

Now it's about sleep.

About sanity.

About professional pride.

Apple understands this instinctively. When speaking about privacy, they don't lead with policy language. They talk about your photos. Your messages. Your life.

The issue becomes personal.

People care when they can see themselves in the outcome not theoretically, but immediately.

Identity Does More Work Than Incentives

Inside organizations, identity is the accelerant leaders underestimate.

Some teams see themselves as:

- The team that fixes things
- The team that never misses deadlines
- The team that protects each other

When new behavior aligns with identity, adoption feels natural.

When it conflicts, incentives rarely fix it.

Slack didn't spread because it was just a better inbox. It spread because using it signaled: *We are a modern, collaborative team.*

Adoption became identity-based.

Once behavior reinforces identity, enforcement becomes unnecessary.

People self-correct.

Stories Do What Dashboards Can't

Data informs.

Stories move.

One honest story a failed customer call, a teammate burning out, a moment of courage travels further than a dozen metrics. Stories transform abstraction into lived experience.

That's why candid retrospectives matter.

And why sanitized success stories fall flat.

People debate numbers.

They remember stories.

Caring Spreads When It's Visible

Caring grows faster when it's social.

Spotify's Wrapped succeeds not just because it's clever, but because it turns private behavior into shared identity. People share it because it reflects something they're proud of, not because a company asked them to.

Inside organizations, the same principle applies:

- Visible effort legitimizes participation.
- Shared learning makes participation safer.
- Public contribution invites replication.

Peer recognition often carries more weight than top-down praise. Internal communities outperform formal mandates.

Caring is contagious, but only when it can be seen.

Give People Something to Hold

People don't want to watch change.

They want a role in it.

The most effective initiatives don't ask everyone to do everything. They offer small, clear entry points:

- Pilot groups
- Rotating facilitators
- Champion networks
- Specific, bounded contributions

Participation converts belief into commitment especially when the role feels manageable.

Ownership grows through action.

When Caring Lasts

Caring endures when:

- The story stays consistent
- Identity is reinforced
- Progress is visible
- People feel seen rather than managed

Movements outlast campaigns.
Cultures outlive their founders.

You cannot force people to care.
But when the conditions are right, something shifts.

They stop waiting to be asked.

THINK ABOUT THIS

The Pattern

People engage deeply when they see themselves in the outcome and believe their actions matter.

Reflect on This

When does work feel meaningful rather than procedural?

What makes someone feel connected to a goal?

Pattern Interrupt: Make the Impact Visible

Take one initiative you are currently working on.

Instead of describing the objective, explain the work through the story of a person affected by it.

Notice whether people respond differently when the work becomes human rather than abstract.

Chapter 17

YOUR RIPPLE EFFECT

"We never know which lives we influence, or when, or why."

— Stephen King

Most people think influence requires scale. A title. A platform. A following large enough that strangers ask you to "share your thoughts" on things you never agreed to have thoughts about.

It doesn't.

At work, influence usually comes from something less glamorous: what you do in rooms other people are trapped in with you. Meetings. Message threads. Hallway conversations that start as small talk and somehow end with a decision no one remembers making.

That's where culture forms, not in decks, not in values statements, not in the beautifully branded PDF no one can find two weeks later. Culture forms in behavior people witness and quietly remember.

We assume our actions are private. Or insignificant. Or explainable.

I was just tired.
That meeting was a mess anyway.
I didn't mean it like that.

But in shared systems, nothing is neutral. Every action sends a signal. And once a signal enters a group, it spreads.

Humans don't operate independently at work, no matter how often we say, "I'm just doing my job." We operate socially. Our brains scan the environment, running questions we never say out loud:

Is it safe to speak here?
What happens if I disagree?
Who gets rewarded? Who gets ignored?
Do I need to look busy or actually be useful?

Your behavior answers those questions whether you intend to or not.

That's how culture spreads. Through observation.

Take meetings. In one team, everyone competes to sound confident, even when no one is sure what's happening. Pauses are awkward. Uncertainty is suspicious. Someone says, "Let's align offline," which means, "This is going nowhere, but we're out of time."

In another team, one person says, "I'm not sure yet can we slow this down?" And nothing bad happens. No eye rolls. No career damage. Just a pause. Over time, better questions appear. Not because leadership launched a psychological safety initiative, but because someone tested the room and survived.

The opposite ripple works just as well. When ideas are met with silence, sarcasm, or polite dismissal, people stop offering ideas.

Not because they're disengaged. Because they're efficient.

Why contribute if the system has already signaled that thinking is optional?

Urgency behaves the same way. In some companies, everything is urgent. Emails arrive at 11:47 p.m. marked "quick." Messages say, "Can you jump on a call?" with no context. Calm is interpreted as laziness. Exhaustion becomes a badge of honor.

No one decides this is the culture. It emerges one late-night message, one praised fire drill, one unchallenged panic at a time.

Mistakes tell an even clearer story. In some teams, someone can say, "That one's on me here's what I learned," and the group moves forward smarter. In others, mistakes are buried or dissected until everyone learns the wrong lesson: don't be the one holding the flashlight.

No policy caused this. Behavior did.

Visibility is what turns individual choices into cultural signals. Private behavior changes you. Visible behavior changes the system. That's why platforms like GitHub accelerated collaboration so quickly. They didn't just enable contribution — they made it visible. People could see others participating, which made participation safer.

There's also a threshold most people don't want to cross alone. Few want to be first. They're willing to be early but not isolated. One visible action rarely flips a system, but it moves someone else closer to their line. Once enough people cross it, the behavior feels obvious, as if it had always been allowed.

Change rarely starts with grand gestures. It starts with small, repeatable actions other people can copy without risking themselves. Speak up once. Ask a better question. Admit uncertainty. Resist fake urgency. These aren't personality traits. They're signals. Repeated, they become norms.

You don't get to opt out of influence. Silence is a signal. Inaction is a signal. What you tolerate teaches people what's acceptable. Culture forms whether you shape it or not.

Once you see behavior as ripple-based instead of isolated, the question changes.

It's no longer *Do I have influence?*

It becomes:

What am I teaching accidentally?

Observe Yourself

The Pattern

Small behaviors from leaders can create large ripple effects that shape the culture of an entire organization.

Reflect on This

What signals do your reactions send to others?

What behaviors receive your attention most often?

Pattern Interrupt: Watch Your Attention

For the next week, notice what actions you respond to most in meetings, messages, or feedback.

What people receive attention for often becomes what they repeat.

Notice what behavior your attention might be amplifying.

Section 6
The Future Is Full of Cats (And Algorithms)

Once you understand the mechanics of influence, there's a natural temptation to ask a dangerous question:

How do I use this?

That question isn't wrong. But it's incomplete.

Because influence doesn't stay neutral just because intentions feel good. The same mechanics that help people learn, align, and care can just as easily narrow perspective, suppress dissent, or accelerate harm when scale and speed outrun judgment.

This is the line Big Tech keeps crossing accidentally and sometimes deliberately.

And as AI enters more decisions, more conversations, and more moments of vulnerability, the cost of getting this wrong stops being theoretical.

Influence without accountability doesn't just move people.

It moves them somewhere.

So before we talk about the future, we need to talk about responsibility.

Chapter 18

WHAT GOOD TECH CAN DO

"Technology is best when it brings people together."

— Matt Mullenweg

Most conversations about technology swing between two lazy extremes. On one side, tech is salvation the thing that will fix inefficiency, bias, and human error. On the other, it's the villain hollowing attention spans and wrecking society.

Both miss the point.

Technology doesn't have values. People do. And technology doesn't decide what kind of world we live in, Design choices do. This isn't about what technology can do. It's about what becomes possible when we decide what it should do.

Technology is a multiplier. It doesn't create intent; it amplifies it. A hammer can build a home or shatter a window. An algorithm can surface life-saving insight or spread misinformation at scale. The difference is never the tool. It's what it's optimized for, and which tradeoffs its designers accept.

Good technology doesn't overpower humans. It supports better behavior. It doesn't replace judgment; it strengthens it. And when designed well, it doesn't remove responsibility it clarifies where it belongs.

You can see hints of this in tools we take for granted. Navigation apps like Google Maps and Waze began as convenience faster routes, less stress. But in emergencies, they reroute people away from danger, reduce congestion, adapt as conditions change. Still convenience. But convenience doing something meaningful.

Scale that deliberately. Cities integrating real-time disaster response into navigation. Evacuation routes adjusting based on crowd movement. Alerts guiding behavior calmly instead of triggering panic. Technology optimizing not just efficiency, but safety, without requiring heroics from users.

Inside companies, a similar shift is possible. AI is mostly framed as productivity software: faster writing, faster analysis, faster execution. Useful, but unimaginative. A more interesting possibility is AI as a thinking partner instead of a task replacer.

Some organizations are experimenting at the edges, building systems that surface dissent before groupthink sets in, tools that flag blind spots, and AI that summarizes opposing viewpoints instead of reinforcing the most popular one. Instead of accelerating bad decisions, technology could slow teams down at the right moments.

Imagine meetings where an AI notices the same three voices dominating and flags who hasn't spoken. Or where historical failure patterns surface before decisions are locked in. Or where assumptions are challenged in real time, not in an audit months later. Not surveillance. Behavioral guardrails.

Learning systems offer another glimpse. Most corporate platforms still treat humans like containers: content goes in, completion gets tracked, behavior rarely changes. Duolingo worked because it made progress visible, normalized struggle, and reinforced identity, not compliance.

The same logic could reshape capability building. Systems that nudge practice instead of assigning content. Platforms that reinforce identity over time instead of checking boxes. Technology that builds humans, not just documents them.

Then there's health. Most platforms optimize for engagement because it's measurable time spent, clicks, retention. But engagement says nothing about whether the experience was helpful or healthy.

It's not hard to imagine a future where platforms reward logging off, normalize pauses instead of infinite scroll, and optimize for long-term wellbeing instead of short-term dopamine.

That future isn't unrealistic.
It's unprioritized.

When technology is designed with intention, organizations change in predictable ways. Clarity increases. Noise decreases. Feedback becomes data instead of drama. Bias surfaces earlier, before hierarchy hardens it into "just the way things are."

Technology doesn't replace leadership in those environments. It augments judgment. It makes better behavior easier and worse behavior harder.

None of this requires science fiction. The data, computing power, and behavioral science already exist. What's missing isn't capability.

It's courage.

The future won't be decided by the smartest algorithms.
It will be decided by the values embedded inside them.

Technology will continue to shape behavior.
What remains undecided is whether that influence is careless or considered.

Optimization without judgment doesn't produce truth.
It produces extremes.

Consider the Tool

The Pattern

Technology amplifies human capability, but its impact depends entirely on the intentions and systems guiding its use.

Reflect on This

When does technology improve judgment?

When might it quietly replace thinking?

Pattern Interrupt: Solve It Two Ways

The next time you use a digital tool or AI system to complete a task, try solving the problem yourself first.

Then use the tool.

Compare the results.

Notice how the presence of technology changes the way you approach the problem.

Chapter 19

CAN YOU TRUST AN ALGORITHM?

"What is dangerous is not ignorance, but the illusion of knowledge."

— Stephen Hawking

At some point, almost everyone asks this sometimes aloud, often quietly: Can you trust an algorithm? Can you trust AI?

The question carries hope and unease. Hope that technology can be objective, efficient, fair. Unease that something invisible is making decisions we don't fully understand.

The honest answer is uncomfortable. You shouldn't trust algorithms. You should understand them, govern them, and remain responsible for how they're used. Algorithms don't have judgment. They inherit it.

An algorithm doesn't decide what matters. It optimizes for what it's told to value. If the goal is engagement, it amplifies what holds attention - outrage, fear, novelty. If the goal is efficiency, it removes friction, sometimes at the cost of care. If the goal is profit, it prioritizes what converts fastest. Algorithms don't choose bias. They absorb it from historical data, human decisions, cultural assumptions, and narrow definitions of success.

They don't introduce bias.

They scale it.

Part of the trust problem is presentation. Numbers feel neutral. Dashboards feel factual. Recommendations feel objective. But that sense of neutrality collapses when the data reflects inequity, the metrics are narrow, or the tradeoffs are invisible.

Hiring algorithms made this visible. Companies adopted AI tools to reduce human bias, only to discover the systems learned from decades of uneven hiring patterns. The algorithm didn't discriminate intentionally. It optimized for what "success" had looked like before. The result wasn't fairness. It was automated inheritance.

Another risk isn't malice, it's confidence. Many systems are optimized to sound fluent and helpful, not to know. When reliable information is missing, they generate the most plausible response based on patterns. This is known as hallucination.

The danger isn't obvious misinformation. It's believable misinformation. Humans trust confidence. When a system speaks with certainty, accuracy is often assumed even when it's guessing.

A related drift occurs when AI is trained to be agreeable. Systems reinforced to validate users can slide into sycophancy mirroring beliefs instead of challenging them. What feels like support can quietly become reinforcement, especially when users interpret responses as neutral authority.

Algorithms are exceptionally good at doing exactly what they're told. That's also their limitation. They can identify what people click, what keeps them engaged, what correlates with past success. They cannot decide what should matter, when efficiency causes harm, or when silence is safer than response.

Recommendation systems illustrate this clearly. Platforms optimized for watch time. Outrage outperforms nuance. The system learned what worked. Optimization without judgment doesn't produce truth.

It produces extremes.

The stakes rise when AI enters emotionally sensitive terrain. Conversational systems have been placed into roles requiring care without boundaries, escalation paths, or refusal mechanisms. In a small number of tragic cases, overreliance on AI responses coincided with real-world harm, including suicide. The systems did not intend harm. They lacked context, judgment, and responsibility. AI does not understand despair. It does not recognize crisis. It does not know when to stop talking.

When tools designed for conversation are placed into roles requiring care, the cost of failure becomes human.

Then there's opacity. Modern AI systems learn dynamically and produce outputs without clear causal explanations sometimes in ways even their creators cannot fully unpack. In areas like credit, insurance, and risk scoring, people can be denied opportunities without meaningful explanation. Appeals become difficult. Accountability blurs. Trust erodes.

Overreliance compounds the problem. When systems appear accurate, humans defer even when outputs conflict with common sense. Drivers follow GPS into lakes. Managers defer to scores over lived context. Organizations hide behind "the system said so."

Blind trust isn't trust.

It's abdication.

Which brings us back to the real question.

It isn't *Can you trust an algorithm?*

It's:

Who is responsible when it causes harm?

LOOK UNDER THE HOOD

The Pattern

Algorithms reflect the priorities and biases embedded within them, making it essential for humans to question how decisions are being shaped.

Reflect on This

What assumptions sit behind the metrics your organization tracks?

What behavior might those metrics encourage?

Pattern Interrupt: Question the Metric

Choose one metric your team follows closely.

Ask two questions:

What behavior does this metric reward?

What behavior might it ignore?

Notice how measurement quietly shapes priorities.

Chapter 20

When AI Starts Herding Us

"The real danger is not that computers will begin to think like men, but that men will begin to think like computers."

— Sydney J. Harris

For most of human history, influence moved slowly. Ideas spread through conversation. Social norms formed through observation. Beliefs developed over time tested, challenged, reshaped. Even propaganda required repetition across years, sometimes generations, before it fully took hold.

Artificial intelligence changed the tempo.

Influence is no longer episodic. It no longer arrives in speeches, campaigns, or public declarations and then fades. It now operates continuously in the background, adapting moment by moment, adjusting quietly to whatever holds attention. And when influence becomes continuous, it stops feeling like persuasion and starts feeling like reality.

This is the moment AI shifts from recommending to herding.

Traditional influence was blunt. A message was created, distributed widely, and hoped to land through a memo, advertisement, or speech. AI-driven influence works differently. It listens first. It observes what captures attention, what reassures, what irritates, what makes someone linger. Then it adjusts. Not once, but constantly.

Two people can interact with the same system and experience entirely different outcome not because of ideology, but because of responsiveness. The system is not asking, *What should people believe?* It is asking, *What keeps this person moving?*

That distinction matters.

When influence adapts to individuals rather than audiences, it becomes harder to detect. There is no obvious moment of persuasion, no clear line where choice ends and guidance begins.

Personalization sounds harmless even generous. It promises convenience: fewer irrelevant results, better recommendations, smoother experiences. At first, that is exactly what it provides.

But personalization has a tipping point.

Initially, it reflects preference. Over time, it begins shaping expectation. What appears repeatedly feels normal. What disappears from view fades from consideration. Alternatives do not vanish dramatically; they simply stop showing up.

Gradually, direction emerges.

This isn't about intent. Repetition combined with responsiveness produces conditioning. The system learns what drives engagement, and engagement becomes a proxy for relevance, importance, even truth. Eventually, something feels obvious not because it has been examined, but because it has been reinforced.

AI systems do not understand emotions. But they are highly effective at recognizing patterns of reaction. They detect when users are tired, bored, anxious, or receptive. Content adjusts accordingly, timing itself to emotional windows that were never consciously opened.

This is not speculative. It is how engagement optimization works.

The danger is not that AI "knows" you. It does not. The danger is that it knows how people like you tend to respond and treats those tendencies as levers.

When influence aligns with emotional states instead of deliberate choice, autonomy does not disappear through force. It thins through momentum.

Here is what makes this especially unsettling: it does not feel like control. It feels like guidance.

Choices still exist, but they become easier in one direction than another. Friction disappears where movement is preferred and quietly reappears where it is not. Pauses shorten. Reflection begins to feel inefficient.

By the time you question whether a decision was freely made, the path has already been smoothed.

This is herding without visible pressure. Direction without explicit command.

Historically, herding required intent. Someone was responsible. Someone could be questioned or removed.

AI herds differently. There is no single shepherd. No clear authority. Direction emerges from aggregated engagement signals optimized and re-optimized at scale. The system responds, adapts, and amplifies without consciously deciding where the herd should go.

The movement feels organic. The outcome often does not.

Influence exists, but responsibility isn't clearly owned.

When influence becomes persistent and adaptive, it does more than shape behavior. It shapes identity.

People begin to understand themselves through the content they consistently see, the communities they are algorithmically guided toward, and the beliefs that are continually affirmed. Micro-identities form faster than reflection can keep pace.

This is how polarization accelerates without overt radicalization.

How nuance fades without being attacked.

How certainty hardens without explicit intent.

Not because people suddenly became extreme, but because ambiguity performs poorly in systems optimized for engagement.

And this does not remain confined to screens.

AI already influences hiring decisions, performance evaluations, credit scoring, insurance pricing, and access to opportunity. As these systems move deeper into daily life, herding becomes less visible and more consequential.

When algorithms quietly determine who gets heard, promoted, flagged, or ignored, influence becomes infrastructure.

And infrastructure, once embedded, is hard to question.

One of the most dangerous assumptions is that AI-driven influence is neutral simply because it is data-driven.

Data does not remove values. It obscures them.

Every system embeds assumptions about what matters, what success looks like, and which trade-offs are acceptable.

When those assumptions go unexamined, momentum begins to feel inevitable.

It isn't.

It's designed.

A Moment of Awareness

The Pattern

AI does not simply process information. It increasingly shapes behavior, attention, and decision-making at scale.

Reflect on This

How much of your online experience is selected for you?

What perspectives might your algorithmic environment filter out?

Pattern Interrupt: The Algorithm Pause

For one day, avoid clicking recommended articles or videos.

Instead choose sources intentionally.

Notice whether your choices differ from what the algorithm usually shows you.

Chapter 21

The World Needs More Shepherds

"The best leaders are those the people hardly know exist. When their work is done, the people say, 'We did it ourselves.'"

— Lao Tzu

For most of human history, leadership was visible. You could point to it, name it, hold it accountable. Kings ruled from thrones. Generals led from the front lines. CEOs directed from corner offices. Influence flowed through identifiable people, titles, and institutions. Even when leadership failed, responsibility had an address.

That clarity is fading.

Today, influence rarely belongs to a single person, and it does not require formal authority to operate. It appears as defaults, rankings, recommendations, nudges, and invisible systems that determine what is easy, what is visible, and what quietly disappears. Power did not vanish. It dispersed.

And that dispersion has created a leadership gap we have not fully acknowledged.

In a world shaped by algorithms, architecture often matters more than authority. A leader can issue directives, but cannot command attention the way they once could. Compliance can be mandated. Belief cannot. Policies can be written. But policies struggle to compete with systems that shape decisions long before anyone pauses to evaluate them.

This is why many traditional leadership tools feel ineffective. People are not necessarily rejecting authority. They are being continuously influenced elsewhere—by systems operating outside meeting rooms and organizational charts.

Leadership today is less about instructing people what to do and more about shaping the environments in which their choices are made.

This is where the distinction between rulers and shepherds becomes essential.

Rulers rely on power. Shepherds rely on responsibility.

A ruler directs from above. A shepherd moves alongside—observing the terrain, sensing danger, adjusting pace, guiding movement without force. Shepherds do not confuse control with care. They understand a fundamental truth: movement will happen regardless. The only question is whether it will be guided intentionally or left to momentum.

Shepherding is quieter than ruling. It is also more demanding.

When influence becomes invisible, the absence of stewardship becomes dangerous. Algorithms do not evaluate whether outcomes are healthy. Markets do not pause to consider long-term consequences. Systems optimize relentlessly for whatever they are rewarded to pursue regardless of who is excluded or what is eroded along the way.

Without individuals willing to ask difficult questions, slow processes down, and design with consequences in mind, direction defaults to whatever scales fastest. And what scales fastest is rarely what is wisest.

The metaphor of shepherding is often misunderstood. It is not softness. It is not passivity. Shepherds do not micromanage, but neither do they abdicate responsibility. They establish boundaries. They create safe pathways. They intervene when conditions become unsafe. The goal is not obedience. It is wellbeing.

In modern systems, shepherding looks like challenging metrics that reward harm. Restoring friction where unchecked speed creates risk. Protecting people affected by decisions they did not consent to and may not even see.

This is not gentle leadership. It is disciplined leadership.

And it is not reserved for CEOs or policymakers alone. Responsibility belongs to anyone who designs systems that shape human behavior: product managers choosing defaults, data scientists selecting training data, executives defining success metrics, educators designing learning environments, founders building platforms, parents setting norms, community leaders shaping culture.

If your decisions influence how others move, choose, learn, or belong, you are already shaping a herd. The question is whether you are doing so consciously.

The future does not need more individuals attempting to dominate systems. It needs more people willing to care for them. Care appears as restraint. As accountability. As the courage to say, *Just because we can does not mean we should.*

It requires accepting responsibility even when recognition is absent and rewards are delayed.

Shepherds understand something rulers often resist: responsibility without applause. When outcomes are positive, the system receives credit. When outcomes fail, the shepherd steps forward.

Ethical leadership in an algorithmic age is not about moral perfection. It is about presence remaining attentive to unintended consequences, to edge cases, to those without power or voice, and to the long arc beyond quarterly results or engagement spikes.

Because influence does not disappear when no one appears to be in charge.

It simply goes uncared for.

Look Around

The Pattern

In complex systems, leadership is less about control and more about guiding direction, protecting values, and helping people move together.

Reflect on This

Where do you hold influence that you might underestimate?

What systems around you could benefit from more intentional guidance?

Pattern Interrupt: Shift the Environment

Identify one small routine in your environment such as how a meeting begins, how feedback is given, or how ideas are shared.

Change one element.

Notice how the environment influences behavior once the structure changes.

SECTION 7
IT WAS NEVER ABOUT CATS

After everything we've examined, it would be easy to end with prescriptions. With warnings. With a checklist of what needs fixing.

But that would miss the point.

The most powerful influence you possess was never at the scale of platforms or policies. It has always been quieter than that. Smaller. Closer.

It exists in the moments when you notice a pattern forming and decide whether to interrupt it.

In the meetings where you choose clarity over speed.

In the systems you participate in, design, tolerate, or quietly reinforce.

Real influence is rarely dramatic. It doesn't announce itself. It shows up in defaults you question, metrics you challenge, assumptions you refuse to leave unexamined.

This was never really about cats.

It was about what happens once you begin to see the invisible forces shaping behavior and recognize that you are not merely subject to them.

You are participating in them.

And participation, once seen, becomes responsibility.

Chapter 22

Once You See It

"In the end, we see what we are ready to see."

— Anonymous

At some point, after hearing the title of this book, someone asked me what kind of cats I meant. Domesticated cats? Big cats? Wild ones?

The honest answer is all of the above and none of the above.

Not the four-legged kind. At least, not literally.

What I've been talking about this whole time are the human kind. Independent. Opinionated. Resistant to being managed. And strangely predictable once you stop trying to control them.

And increasingly, the digital kind too, systems and algorithms that behave less like machines and more like self-reinforcing creatures of habit.

Cats simply turned out to be the easiest way to talk about something we don't love admitting about ourselves: independence doesn't disappear in groups. Control is mostly an illusion. And people rarely move because they were told to.

They move because something in their environment made movement feel obvious, reasonable, or inevitable.

Everything in this book has circled that idea from different angles.

We began with the forces that shape belief before intention ever arrives, repetition, convenience, and algorithms quietly deciding what feels familiar or true. Then we moved closer, into teams and organizations, where the same mechanics show up through meetings, incentives, and culture, just with better lighting and worse coffee.

Eventually, we widened the lens again toward technology and AI, where those same dynamics now operate faster, more personally, and at a scale we are still learning to understand.

Different settings. Same pattern.

Most of the time, it is ambient, embedded in defaults, reinforced through repetition, strengthened by what gets rewarded or ignored on an ordinary Tuesday afternoon.

That's why so many well-intentioned efforts fall flat. Not because people are lazy or resistant, but because behavior does not change through instruction alone.

It changes through environment.

Culture does not live in statements. Leadership does not live in titles. Values do not live in slides.

They live in what actually happens when no one is performing for the room.

One persistent mistake is assuming influence begins the moment someone decides to lead. In reality, it usually starts much earlier, in how choices are framed, how friction is removed, how meaning quietly accumulates over time.

Once you begin to see that, familiar frustrations make more sense: why people agree enthusiastically and then disengage; why initiatives stall despite momentum; why technology feels both powerful and unsettling at the same time.

It is not confusion.

It is design.

And design matters more now than ever. As systems grow more intelligent and more personalized, influence becomes easier to deploy and harder to detect. The same tools that help people learn, connect, and create can just as easily narrow perspective, amplify emotion, and shape behavior at scale.

The technology itself is not the villain.

The absence of intention is.

Which brings me back, one last time, to the cats.

Cats do not follow commands particularly well. But they do follow patterns. They respond to environments that make sense to them. They resist force instinctively. They adapt quickly when conditions shift.

Humans are not very different.

When behavior aligns with identity, effort feels reasonable, and meaning is clear, movement happens without coercion. When it doesn't, no amount of messaging closes the gap.

That is not cynicism.

It is realism.

If there is a single thread in this book, it is not control or persuasion.

It is attention.

Attention to how systems shape behavior.

Attention to what is being normalized.

Attention to the small decisions that quietly accumulate into culture, trust, and direction.

In the end, this was never really a book about cats.

It was about understanding how humans move through the world as it actually is, influenced, social, imperfect, and deeply responsive to design.

Once you see that, leadership looks different.
Technology looks different.
Responsibility definitely looks different.

And once you see it,
it's very hard to unsee.

A Different Lens

The Pattern

Once we begin to recognize the systems shaping behavior, leadership becomes less about reacting and more about intentionally shaping environments.

Reflect on This

What patterns from this book now appear in your daily work?

Where does behavior look less random and more systemic?

Pattern Interrupt: Pattern Spotting

For one week, keep a short list of moments when you notice group behavior influencing decisions.

Notice how similar patterns appear in very different situations.

The 30-Day Herding Cats Experiment

If you're curious what happens when you start paying closer attention to influence and systems, try a few of the experiments from this book over the next month.

You don't need to do all of them. Simply choose a few and observe what happens.

The goal is not to change everything at once. It's to begin noticing the invisible forces that shape behavior inside organizations and groups.

Here is one way to explore the ideas over the next thirty days.

Week 1 - Notice Alignment

Try two small observations this week.

- Ask colleagues to write down the team's top priority in one sentence. Compare the answers.
- At the end of a meeting, ask everyone what they are taking away from the conversation.

Notice where alignment exists and where assumptions were hiding.

Week 2 - Watch Behavior

This week, focus on the signals people receive.

- Notice which actions receive praise or recognition.
- Pay attention to what leaders respond to most quickly.

Observe what behavior the system quietly rewards.

Week 3 - Examine the Structure

Now shift your attention to systems.

- Walk through one everyday process step by step.
- Ask what behavior the design of the system makes easiest.

Notice how structure shapes decisions.

Week 4 - Try a Small Change

Finally, experiment with a small shift.

- Change one routine in your environment.
- Begin a meeting differently, ask a new question, or adjust how ideas are shared.

Watch how people respond when the environment changes.

FIELD NOTES

If you try one of the experiments in this book and notice something interesting, I would be curious to hear what you observe.

Across industries and organizations, similar patterns of influence and group behavior appear in very different environments. When people start paying attention, those patterns become easier to recognize.

If you would like to share something you noticed, visit:

DeepaKartha.com

Once there, go to the **Books** section and look for **The Art and Science of Herding Cats**. You'll find a place there to share your observation and read what others are noticing as they try these ideas in their own environments.

From time to time I also share a short synthesis of patterns readers are discovering.

Participation is optional.

But paying attention is where change begins.

Further Reading

This is a collection of books readers might find interesting if they would like to explore some of the ideas and themes discussed here in greater depth.

Influence, Propaganda, and Media

Benkler, Y., Faris, R., & Roberts, H. (2018). *Network propaganda: Manipulation, disinformation, and radicalization in American politics.* Oxford University Press.

Chomsky, N. (2002). *Media control: The spectacular achievements of propaganda.* Seven Stories Press.

Kakutani, M. (2018). *The death of truth: Notes on falsehood in the age of Trump.* Tim Duggan Books.

Marantz, A. (2019). *Antisocial: Online extremists, techno-utopians, and the hijacking of the American conversation.* Viking.

Wardle, C., & Derakhshan, H. (2017). *Information disorder: Toward an interdisciplinary framework for research and policy making.* Council of Europe.

Evidence for Democracy. (2023). *Annotated bibliography for online misinformation and disinformation.* Evidence for Democracy.

Echo Chambers, Algorithms, and Ease

Cinelli, M., et al. (2021). The echo chamber effect on social media. *Proceedings of the National Academy of Sciences, 118*(9).

Fogg, B. J. (2009). A behavior model for persuasive design. In *Proceedings of the 4th International Conference on Persuasive Technology.*

Fogg, B. J. (2019). *Tiny habits: The small changes that change everything.* Houghton Mifflin Harcourt.

Vosoughi, S., Roy, D., & Aral, S. (2018). The spread of true and false news online. *Science, 359*(6380), 1146–1151.

Groupthink, Herd Behavior, and Decisions

Janis, I. L. (1982). *Groupthink: Psychological studies of policy decisions and fiascoes* (2nd ed.). Houghton Mifflin.

Janis, I. L. (1998). Groupthink, Bay of Pigs, and Watergate reconsidered. *Review of General Psychology, 2*(3), 175–187.

U.S. Army Command and General Staff College. (1997). *Effects of groupthink on tactical decision-making.* U.S. Army Command and General Staff College.

Franklin D. Roosevelt Presidential Library and Museum. (1933–1944). *Fireside chats of Franklin D. Roosevelt.* National Archives and Records Administration.

About the Author

Deepa Kartha works at the intersection of leadership, behavioral science, and execution systems.

Her work focuses on a deceptively simple question: why do capable organizations struggle to execute clearly, especially in environments defined by speed, complexity, and AI-driven change?

Over the past two decades, Deepa has worked across engineering leadership, transformation initiatives, and enterprise program design. Through that work she began noticing a recurring pattern: most organizations do not suffer from a lack of strategy or capability. They suffer from **decision friction**—unclear ownership, ambiguous escalation paths, and invisible behavioral signals that quietly slow execution.

Today her work focuses on helping organizations reduce that friction and embed behavior change directly into daily work.

Deepa is the creator of **Decision Velocity Architecture**, a framework designed to install structural clarity around decision ownership, escalation thresholds, time boundaries, and override protocols inside AI-accelerated organizations.

She is also the founder of two platforms designed to activate transformation from both sides of the operating system:

Journyz — The Business Operating System

A platform that translates strategy into execution by structuring workflows, accountability, escalation logic, and cross-team coordination.

CultureRox — The Human Operating System

A behavior-based system that activates leadership habits, culture change, and AI-era readiness through daily micro-practices, peer reinforcement, and measurable engagement.

Together these platforms help organizations align strategy, systems, and human behavior so that change becomes a lived operating rhythm rather than a presentation.

Deepa writes and speaks widely about leadership, execution clarity, and organizational behavior in the age of AI. Her newsletter, **Keep Calm and Tech On**, explores how leaders navigate complexity, influence systems, and design environments where behavior change actually sticks.

Her speaking and advisory work focuses on topics such as:

- Decision Friction in the Age of AI
- Why Execution Fails Even When Strategy Is Clear
- Activating the Human Operating System
- From Escalation Inflation to Decision Clarity

Deepa holds an MBA from the Kellogg School of Management at Northwestern University and a degree in Computer Science and Engineering.

Outside of her work with organizations, Deepa's curiosity about human systems shows up in other ways. She has taught yoga and dance for many years, enjoys gardening, and is endlessly fascinated by how people interact, collaborate, and influence one another, sometimes most clearly when observed from a distance.

Those observations eventually became the foundation for this book.

If the ideas in this book resonate with you, you can explore more of Deepa's work, writing, and speaking at:

DeepaKartha.com

CultureRox — **culturerox.com**

Journyz — **journyz.com**

www.ingramcontent.com/pod-product-compliance
Lightning Source LLC
LaVergne TN
LVHW090526110826
845146LV00003B/1000

* 9 7 9 8 9 9 5 2 8 4 9 1 8 *